WHY NOT BE HAPPY?

THE CHOICE IS YOURS

BRIAN D. MOSBY

Why Not Be Happy?: The Choice is Yours

ISBN: 978-1-63945-698-7 (sc)
ISBN: 978-1-63945-699-4 (e)

Writers' Branding
1-800-608-6550
www.writersbranding.com
media@writersbranding.com

This book is not intended to diagnose or disregard illnesses, conditions or disorders that require professional help. It is not considered a substitute for medication or professional treatment.

In Loving Memory Vera E. Mosby
1940-1975

CONTENTS

INTRODUCTION

The epic search continues. People still chase happiness like a dog chases its tail. But happiness is not that elusive. In fact, to use the phrase that it's right under one's nose still suggests that it's further away than it really is. In fact, true happiness comes from the inside. So what's the point of reading this book if we've already established where happiness comes from? Because I can tell you that money comes from the Federal Reserve, but unless you learn to generate money for yourself, knowing about the Federal Reserve isn't going to do you much good. This book exposes popular misconceptions about what generates happiness. It also shows you how to conquer those negative giants in your life that are rooted in fear. I believe that a Ford mechanic is the best person to work on a Ford vehicle. I believe that Colonel Sanders' recipe is the best one to use if you want to make Kentucky Fried Chicken. I also believe that the best person to lead you into happiness is the Word of God. I refer to Jesus Christ as the Word of God because of John 1:1, "In the beginning was the Word, and the Word was with God and the Word was God." And on verse 14, "The Word became flesh and made his dwelling among us." Don't worry. You don't need an extensive grasp of the Bible to benefit from this book; however, to get the most value out of this book you should make the Word the final authority in your life. I'm not a pastor, deacon, or altar boy. I'm someone who has been inspired by the Holy Spirit to write this book. Although we may all come from different backgrounds, I believe that true happiness begins by making Jesus the Lord of your life. This book will not push religion, but rather, you will be pushed to confront your demons and become more than a conqueror. So if you're ready for the challenge of change, press on!

I

Why Should I Be Happy?

From this point on, I would like us to have a clear understanding of what this book defines as "happiness." ***Happiness is relaxing in peace, enjoying the prosperity of the soul, and trusting in blessed assurances.*** Sound too good to be true? It won't, after you've read this book. Notice that happiness is active and not passive. It's something you do, not something that happens to you. Happiness is relaxing, enjoying, and trusting. This correctly implies that happiness is a journey and not a destination. It's something you actively incorporate into your everyday life, not a destination that you may or may not reach someday. Jesus says in John 16:33, "These things I have spoken to you, that in Me you may have peace. In the world, you will have tribulation; but be of good cheer, I have overcome the world." Jesus commands us to be of good cheer. In other words, cheer up! He understands that there will be bad times, but He wants us to cheer up and be happy anyway. This verse also implies that it is within our power to choose happiness. Jesus wouldn't tell you to do something if He knew you couldn't do it. The difficulty for most people is discovering exactly how to do it. We will come back to John 16:33 because it's so powerful. For now let's break down the definition of happiness and how to attain it.

Relaxing in Peace

Be careful not to confuse excitement with happiness. Yes, you can be excited and happy at the same time, but excitement is not happiness. Excitement is largely emotional. It comes and it goes. It is usually triggered by an outside circumstance. Happiness derives from a conscious, mindful effort. It is constant and it is triggered by you. See the difference? One of the key indicators of happiness is a relaxed state of mind. Sometimes you can actually see happiness on someone's face. Imagine for a moment the look of a happy person. How would you describe them? If you made a list of five words to describe what a happy person looks like, "relaxed" would most likely be on your list, wouldn't it? That's because happy people have no worries. Everyone has concerns, but worrying is a different subject all together that we will discuss in more detail when we talk about overcoming fear. Anxiety and peace are opposites. You can't be anxious (full of worries) and at peace (with no worries) at the same time. In fact, the Bible instructs us in Philippians 4:6, to "Be anxious for nothing, but in everything by prayer and supplication, with thanksgiving, let your request be made known to God." By trusting in God to hear and answer our prayers, we begin to achieve peace. What should you be praying about? Everything that concerns you. By bringing your concerns to God in prayer, you don't allow your concerns to become worries. And if you don't have worries, you can have peace. If you haven't done so yet, it's time to develop a relationship with God. You need to be able to trust in His goodness, power, and His wisdom. The way you develop a relationship with God begins by getting into the Word. By reading the Bible every day, even if it's only a verse or two, you begin to understand the love that God has for you. Think about how easy it is to trust someone who deeply loves you, has your best interest at heart, and has the power to control the universe. Here's a mental picture for you:

God's hands are cupped and full of water. You're floating on a rubber raft in that same water. God is smiling down at you and He's pleased with you. You're relaxing in peace.

Enjoying the Prosperity of the Soul

What is the soul and how does it prosper? The "soul" consists of the mind, will, and emotions. The "mind" refers to your intellect, your ability to think, reason, and analyze. It is in the mind that we define happiness. This is why it's so important to evaluate the way we perceive things. Our perceptions guide our thinking. If we have false and negative perceptions, we will have false and negative thoughts. And the old adage is true: Your thoughts become your words, and your words become your actions, and your actions become your character, and your character becomes your destiny. It all begins in the mind. So what is mental prosperity? It is the ability to maintain healthy, constructive thoughts. This goes beyond the concept of positive thinking. Paul tells us in 2 Corinthians 10:4-5, "For the weapons of our warfare are not carnal but mighty in God for pulling down strongholds, casting down arguments and every high thing that exalts itself against the knowledge of God, bringing every thought into captivity to the obedience of Christ." The war between good and evil takes place on the battlefield of the mind. If we control our minds (our thoughts), we control our destiny. Destructive habits, anger, fear, and anxiety develop first in the mind and can be controlled in the mind. Satan attacks our mind by bombarding us with negative, destructive thoughts. He uses deception to draw us away from God. He wants you to trust in yourself, not God. He wants you to "believe it when you see it," and not have faith in Almighty God. He has deceived us in so many ways it's hard to even realize. I'm glad that God has given us direction in terms of what things we should be mindful of. "Finally, brethren, whatever things are true, whatever things are noble, whatever things are just, whatever things are pure, whatever things are lovely, whatever things are of good report, if there is any virtue and if there is anything praise worthy-meditate on these things." (Philippians 4:8).

How can your will prosper? By getting your will in line with the will of God. How do we determine God's will? By getting in the Word. By reading the Bible, we learn about God and His promises, or blessed assurances, for us. God has given each one of us free will. "I have set before you life and death, blessing and cursing; therefore choose life, that both you and your descendants shall live." (Deuteronomy 30:19). We can choose an ungodly, destructive life. We can choose to disbelieve all His promises. In fact, we don't even have to do what He wants us to do. We can do whatever we want. God made it that way. We can either live a life full of blessings or curses. It amazes me that people choose to live life by their own set of rules, doing what they want when they want and still end up miserable. It's like a teenager who despises his parents for making him work, giving him chores, preparing healthy meals for him to eat, guiding him into education, church, and family responsibility. A parent knows that these are the best things for the child. A parent knows that in the end the child will be well prepared for whatever life throws their way. Rarely do teenagers see it that way. God's will is for you to prosper. He knows what's best for you. He wants you to be on one accord with Him. He wants your will to be in line with His.

How can you prosper emotionally? "Emotional prosperity" has two components. The first component is about control and the second component is about release. We attain emotional prosperity by first controlling our destructive emotions and not letting our destructive emotions control us. This does not mean stifling or suppressing your emotions. We are emotional beings and we can't stop having emotions. We can, however, control our exercise of these emotions. This means not allowing that anger to explode. It means not allowing yourself to wallow in self-pity. It means not allowing fear and doubts to take residence in your mind. The second component is about releasing God's joy in your life. Jesus prays in John 17:13, "But now I come to You, and these things I speak in the world, that they may have My joy fulfilled in themselves." One of the basic functions of God's Word is to fill you with joy! When you mentally take hold of that, you will be eager to get into the Word because that's where you find your joy.

So we see that enjoying the prosperity of your soul involves enjoying mental prosperity, by maintaining healthy and Word-inspired thoughts. It involves getting our will in line with God's will by developing our knowledge of God's will through His Word and aligning our will with His. And finally it involves enjoying emotional prosperity by managing our emotions and being filled with joy through God's Word.

Trusting in Blessed Assurances

God's Word is full of promises that serve to sustain you, give you joy, raise your spirit, give you strength, and give you peace. Here are some examples of some of these blessed assurances:

- John 3:16, "For God so loved the world that He gave his only begotten Son, that whoever believes in Him should not perish but have everlasting life."
- Matthew 6:25-26, "Therefore I say unto you, do not worry about your life, what you will eat or what you will drink, nor about your body, what you will put on. Is not life more than food and the body more than clothing? Look at the birds of the air, for they neither sow nor reap nor gather into barns; yet your heavenly Father feeds them. Are you not of more value than they?"

- ❖ Psalm 91:11-12, "For He shall give his angels charge over you, to keep you in all your ways. They shall bear you up in their hands, lest you dash your foot against a stone."
- ❖ Philippians 4:13, "I can do all things through Christ who strengthens me."
- ❖ Romans 8:38-39, "For I am persuaded that neither death nor life, nor angels nor principalities nor powers, nor things present nor things to come, nor height nor depth, nor any other created thing, shall be able to separate us from the love of God which is in Christ Jesus our Lord."
- ❖ Psalm 136:1, "Oh give thanks to the Lord, for He is good! For His mercy endures forever."
- ❖ Psalm 103:12, "As far as the east is from the west, so far has He removed our transgressions from us."

Obviously we're not going to list them all, but these are seven powerful scriptures on which you can lay most any burden. These seven blessed assurances are cornerstones to building happiness and they've helped me stay balanced. You may have seven scriptures of your own or you may adopt these seven as your personal blessed assurances. The point is to have a few inspiring scriptures in your heart so that you can draw on them at will. Let's take a closer look at these scriptures and see their significance.

John 3:16 is one of the most popular scriptures in the world. It highlights God's love for us. God loved us so much that He allowed His only Son to be a living sacrifice for our sins. God knew what had to be done to redeem man from his fall in the Garden of Eden. Adam had messed it up for everybody. We were separated from our true godly nature when Adam disobeyed God. At that point, God could have said, "OK, you don't want to listen to me, have it your way. You and your descendants are cursed forever. I don't need you, you need Me. This is just the beginning of your shortcomings. I will leave man and never help him again because he has disobeyed Me." But God didn't take that approach. He said, "I love you and I'm gonna put you back in right-standing with Me. One man messed it up, and one man will make it right. The only man for the job is someone not born of man but born of Me. His life will be sacrificed for all. His blood will wash away all sins. By His stripes all will be healed, because I love you." Praise God! For He so loved the world that He gave His only begotten Son to bring salvation for the world.

Matthew 6:25-26 is one of the main reasons we shouldn't sweat the small stuff. This verse is basically saying that there are more important things in life that should concern you. God will take care of your basic necessities so don't worry about it. Sounds simple but how many times do we let these things consume us? We allow ourselves to worry about fads, the latest gossip, and keeping up with the Joneses. Instead of being consumed with the outside of people and things, we should be concerned about the inside of people and being closer to God. If we can redirect our focus, we will realize that there's a lifetime of spiritual work to be done. Quitting that bad habit, experiencing God's Word, praying more effectively, learning how to hear from God, being in fellowship with other Christians, encouraging one another, doing God's will, and the list goes on. Don't waste your time focusing on basic necessities and secular talk. God supplies our every need and He's given us a journey called life for development.

Psalm 91:11-12 provides us with the peace of mind of knowing that heavenly hosts guard our physical well- being. Have you ever seen the president walking to a facility surrounded by big men with radios and guns? Picture yourself being surrounded by those big men who would follow you wherever you go. That would make you feel pretty secure, wouldn't it? Now instead of being surrounded by big men, picture yourself surrounded by mighty angels whose strength and physical capabilities far exceed any human being. Their orders are to protect you from seen and unseen danger. How does that make you feel? This is just a taste of what God has already provided for those who have made Him the Lord of their lives and who trust in Him.

Philippians 4:13 illustrates what power you have through Jesus Christ. This verse is the reason why the word "can't" should not be a part of your vocabulary. This verse is the reason why you should have complete confidence that you will overcome your demons. This verse requires faith and patience and it will drive any doubts or fears of failure that you may have once had. Believe it so you can achieve it.

Romans 8:38-39 eliminates any guilt that you may be feeling about yourself because God still loves you in spite of you. God's love is not human. His love is not conditional or fleeting. God hates sin. He has the power to wash away your sins and love you as if your sins never existed. This verse also eliminates any fear that someone can separate you from God's love. Satan can deceitfully influence you to turn your face away from God, but you have the power to choose. God gave you that power and no one can take it away. Remember Philippians 4:13? When we feel separated from God, it's not Him that turns His face away from us. Love God the way He loves you: without conditions, through good times and bad, and without fear or doubts. Nothing can separate you from the love of God.

Psalm 136:1 is so powerful. You should pick up a Bible and read the entire chapter of Psalm 136 today. God's mercy endures forever. You may say, "But what about my past, what about those terrible things I've done?" God's mercy endures forever. God hates sin. When you sin, you should repent, or be remorseful and turn away, from your sin and come boldly before God to receive mercy. He doesn't run out of mercy. There's not a limited supply of it. God's mercy endures forever.

Psalm 103:12 is another guilt eliminator. Once you truly get this scripture in your heart, you will no longer feel guilty about those times when you stumbled and fell. You will instead be quick to get back up on your feet and continue the spiritual battle until the day of glory. God's not waiting to pound you over the head with a list of all the sins you've ever committed. He's waiting for you to accept Him as your personal Savior. He's waiting for you to receive His mercy and His grace. He's waiting at the door of your heart so that He can come in. He's waiting to remove your sins as far away from you as the east is from the west. Now who can measure that?

Tuck these blessed assurances away in your heart, and you'll always have sustaining ammunition. The more Word you have, the more sustenance you'll have. This is not about memorizing seven scriptures. It is about making the Word the final authority in your life and having faith in what you read. The Bible defines "faith" as the substance of things hoped for and the evidence of things not seen (Hebrews 11:1). So read these scriptures over and over again, until you know them to be true in your heart.

Up to this point we have defined happiness and looked at each element of its definition. ***Happiness is relaxing in peace, enjoying the prosperity of the soul, and trusting in blessed assurances.*** It is a way of life we actively choose. It begins by seeking God through His Word and it is maintained by walking with God daily. This requires an active prayer life and continued growth in His Word. So choose God and choose happiness. It's not as difficult as you may think. God's yoke is easy and His burden is light (see Matthew 11:29-30).

World Happiness versus True Happiness

We must be careful not to get confused by what the world considers happiness. When I speak of the world, what I am referring to is that which is natural, carnal, or of the flesh. Our natural human tendencies are to seek our own lustful pleasures and desires. But as Christians we are not to be lead by the flesh, we are to be lead by the spirit. This creates an internal conflict because man is a triune being. He is spirit, soul, and body. When we accept Jesus as our Lord and personal Savior, our spirit is reborn into the very image of God. What happens next is that our spirit, a new creation, begins to desire spiritual things such as peace, joy, love, harmony, etc. But our flesh still craves carnal things such as pleasures of the flesh, selfishness, greed, etc. So naturally, what makes the flesh happy is going to be different than what makes the spirit happy. "For those who live according to the flesh set their minds on the things of the flesh, but those who live according to the Spirit, the things of the Spirit. For to be carnally minded is death, but to be spiritually minded is life and peace." (Romans 8:5-6). Let's take a look at what the world traditionally considers to bring happiness so that we won't confuse it with true happiness.

Money

This is one of the biggest deceptions on the planet. Satan has many sinners and many believers deceived into thinking that money brings us happiness. We see the lifestyles of the rich, and we think they're happy because of all the money and possessions they have. The truth is that money can't buy you love or happiness. Some may say, "Yeah, Brian, I already know that money doesn't bring you happiness." But it goes deeper than that. We say we already know that money can't bring us happiness yet we live as though we can't be happy without it. We play the lottery faithfully every week but we have problems tithing. We save money in a bank account but we won't give to the poor. We invest in retirement plans but we don't pray to God to meet our every need. We can take a trip to Vegas or Atlantic City but we won't send our relatives money when they need it. In fact, some of us are convinced that we won't be happy until we get that new house or that new car or that new television. We believe money can get us all these things. So the plan becomes, "When I get enough money, I'll buy all those things that I desire and then I'll be happy." Does that sound familiar? It should. It's what most of us have believed at some point in our lives, including myself. The truth is that seeking money to create happiness is foolish. "But those who desire to be rich fall into temptation and a snare, and into many foolish and harmful lusts which drown men in destruction and perdition."(1 Timothy 6:9). We have to start our journey to happiness with God, not with money. "Command those who are rich in this present age not to be haughty, nor to trust in uncertain riches but in the living God, who gives us richly all things to enjoy." (1 Timothy 6:17).

It's not that money is a bad thing in itself. The scriptures say that the love of money is a root of all kinds of evil (1 Timothy 6:10). When you depend on money or any other false god to solve your problems, you open the doorway to all kinds of demonic forces that create havoc in your life. God doesn't want you to live in poverty. He just wants you to cast all your cares on Him so that He can be your strength, your rock, and your salvation. He wants you to trust in Him, not in money.

Perfection

Some people try to achieve happiness by being perfect. They want things to be "right." The thought process here suggests that when things are just right, you have happiness. Therefore I won't be happy until everything is perfect. This is sometimes considered compulsive behavior in the world of psychology, but the ramifications of trying to be perfect go beyond psychology. People who have unfortunately been enslaved by this lifestyle spend their days trying to correct everything from the way the curtains hang to the way their shoes are laced. Some of these individuals focus on having the perfect look, leading the perfect life, or saying the perfect words. There are many variations and subtleties to this way of life, and I'm not a psychologist, but I don't have to be. This way of life focuses on not making mistakes and trying to exist on an unattainable level. Basically, it is a lifestyle rooted in fear. In fact, this behavior may have been caused by some traumatic, fear- inducing event. The game plans for these individuals become focused on having a great defense as the best offence. That may be true in certain sports, but it just doesn't cut it in real life. Remember we said that happiness is active, not passive. It's something you do, not something that happens to you. Happiness won't just magically appear because you haven't made any mistakes. You won't achieve happiness because you've reached some level of perfection. All you're doing when you strive for perfection in worldly terms is avoiding a certain fear. You can't achieve perfection on your own anyway. It is God who perfects. "It is God who arms me with strength, and makes my way perfect." (Psalm 18:32). Until you are reborn and have accepted Jesus as your personal savior with the Holy Spirit dwelling in you, you don't have the power to make your way perfect. But through Christ all things are possible.

Sometimes things stray away from our plans for our own good. We have to learn to trust in God to lead us in whatever situation comes our way. Getting fired could open the door to the best job you'll ever have. Falling down gives you the opportunity to get up. To get up requires strength, determination, and courage. It's not about having things always go according to our plans, as perfect as we may think our plans are. It's about having things go God's way. We need to learn from our mistakes, not avoid them. We should accept Jesus as our personal savior and strive for perfection, realizing that in the end God will perfect us over time. When God has finished His good work in us, we shall come forth as pure gold: sanctified, without blemish, and perfect.

Fame

This desire is probably one of the more subtle things to recognize. "Fame" is defined in *The Random House College Dictionary* as a widespread reputation (especially a good one). Many have sold out to the dark side to obtain this. You may not be a rock star, movie star, or television personality, but maybe you've lusted after fame discreetly or even unknowingly. Let's look at the definition of fame. The word "widespread" doesn't have to be global or nationwide. You could desire a widespread reputation among your family, coworkers or peers. If you've ever met someone who constantly brags about what they've accomplished, cannot admit to being wrong or making a bad decision, craves the limelight, and/or is very self-centered, then you've probably met someone who craves a widespread reputation. This type of person has usually learned to believe that their fame will bring them happiness. They believe that famous people have it good and easy, things just work out for them, and that fame can help them to obtain their hearts desires. So they'll be happy when they become famous and in order to become famous they have to exalt themselves.

Jesus says, "And whoever exalts himself will be abased, and whoever humbles himself will be exalted." (Matthew 23:12). Humility is the key. When we humble ourselves to God, He exalts us. He takes charge of our reputation according to His will. What does humbling ourselves to God mean? It means that we should be careful not to seek our own ambition. It means we should live our lives with the Word as our guide. It means we should be sensitive to the Holy Spirit's direction. It means we should pray about tough decisions and be led by our reborn spirit. It means that God's will should take precedence over our will. It's a high calling with high rewards. The most prosperous lives are being lead by people who have God as their anchor and provider. These individuals lean on Him and trust in Him. They seek a good reputation because they realize that as Christians they are the light of the world. They represent God's grace and righteousness.

There's a difference between a good reputation and a widespread reputation. We should seek a good reputation and let God handle the rest. It's the motive behind your seeking that has God's interest. Are you seeking a good reputation or a widespread one? Sometimes only God knows your true intentions, which is why we should not be quick to judge others but quick to evaluate our own motives. When we walk in love, we know we're OK because we're walking with God.

Licentiousness

"Licentiousness" is defined in the dictionary as, "sexually unrestrained or unrestrained by law or morality." This hedonistic concept is very destructive, as you can imagine. People who adopt this way of life believe that pleasure brings happiness. They believe that by pursuing that which satisfies the flesh, they will achieve happiness. They don't believe in restraints. We've all seen this type of behavior, maybe even in ourselves. Those who have multiple sex partners or those who have had sex many times before marriage would obviously fall into this category. In God's eyes, sex before marriage is destructive anyway. Sex within marriage is what God intended for us and does not fall into this discussion. But the definition of licentiousness includes more than sex. It also refers to behavior that is "unrestrained by law or morality." Those who smoke, eat, or even sleep excessively would also fall into this category. When we look at this a little closer we can actually see why this is a bad philosophy. Remember earlier at the beginning of this chapter when I said that what makes the flesh happy is opposite of what makes the spirit happy. I followed it up with the scripture, Romans 8:5-6. Well, this is what I was talking about. When our flesh is in control, we are in bondage.

When God is in control, we are set free. The flesh and the Spirit are exact opposites! The world believes that when you have the freedom to choose your actions as you see fit, that's freedom. The world believes that when you don't have to listen to anyone but yourself, that's freedom. The world believes that when you're "free" to do whatever you want to do, that's freedom. Nonsense. Satan has cleverly blinded the world into thinking that we should satisfy our flesh because it feels good and that we should have the "freedom" to do whatever we want to do. But thank God for the truth, because the truth shall set you—.

The truth is that God gives you true freedom. He has given us the gift of free will. We can choose him or Satan. "I call heaven and earth as witnesses today against you, that I have set before you life and death, blessing and cursing; therefore choose life, that both you and your descendants may live" (Deuteronomy 30:19). God is so great that he doesn't force you to choose Him. He allows you to make your own choice. Love is the bondage when you choose God. You become one with Him and your will comes in line with His. And after that, you still have a choice to fall from grace and leave Him for Satan. When you choose God, you receive all that comes along with God—peace, love, joy, happiness, etc. When you choose Satan you receive all that comes along with Satan—strife, fear, loneliness, etc. When you choose to satisfy your flesh, your happiness is only temporary. When you choose to satisfy your spirit, your happiness is everlasting. The flesh dies, but the spirit is eternal.

Does Satan give you a choice? What happens when you choose to do whatever you want? What happens when you choose a life of licentiousness? You develop addictions and you become a slave to your flesh. All of a sudden you begin to say things like, "I can't stop smoking." Or "I can't stop drinking." Or "I can't go without sex until I'm married." Why can't you? I thought you were free to do whatever you wanted. The truth is that you are never free when your flesh is in charge. The truth is that the world has been craftily deceived. The truth is that you can't serve two different masters at once. Either you will serve God and be free from the destruction and death that sin brings, or you will serve Satan and indulge in the sins of your flesh, which in the end is death. True freedom can only be attained when you choose God. So choose God. He's waiting for you. Money, perfection, fame, and licentiousness are all examples of external happiness, or happiness without God. The world has been deceived into thinking that happiness can be attained without knowing God when the truth is that He is the author of true happiness. We must stop allowing our flesh to direct our behaviors and put our spirit in charge. For most of us, our flesh is much stronger than our spirit, so when the two compete, the flesh usually wins out. This is because we feed our flesh but we do not feed our spirit. We feed our flesh by entertaining lustful thoughts and feeding our cravings. The battle against the flesh begins in the mind. We have to control our thought life and stop giving in to the desires of the flesh. The flesh is a bottomless pit. You can't do enough to satisfy the flesh. People with smoking habits smoke more and more cigarettes per day as time goes on. People with eating disorders need more and more food to satisfy their appetite. In fact, that was one of my problems. I grew up in a household, like many other households, where more was better when it came to eating. If you went over someone's house and they cooked for you, it was an insult to eat less than two plates. My father was a big strong man with a healthy appetite, so this never posed a problem for him. I wanted to be just like my dad. I inherited his healthy appetite, and I grew up learning how to overeat. My cue to stop eating was when my stomach hurt. That slight pain was the only thing that stopped me from eating after every meal. By the time I was twelve, I could eat more than most adults. Well, my dream of being like my father came true. My father was 6' 1", with broad shoulders, muscles all over, and over 200 lbs. He never looked fat, because he carried his weight well. By the time I was eighteen, I was 5' 11", broad shoulders, muscles all over and over 200 lbs. Except I wasn't carrying my weight as well. I'd had love handles since I was thirteen, and my bulging stomach was always an issue. My blood pressure normally ran high and I couldn't run one lap around a track without being exhausted. My appetite never decreased because I perpetuated the problem by continuing to overeat after every meal. I was practicing a lifestyle based on licentiousness. I was gonna eat what I wanted, when I wanted, and how much I wanted. It wasn't until I understood that I was being a glutton—thanks to an old college buddy named Gene—that I changed my eating habits. And as you can imagine it was very difficult being that I had been overeating for more than twenty years. The more I understood biblically about gluttony, lust of the flesh, and being spirit lead, the easier it was for me to commit to making a change. It takes time and commitment to make a permanent lifestyle change. It also takes feeding your spirit by getting into the Word. As your spirit grows, your flesh weakens. To be spiritually strong is the first step in gaining true happiness. Now that we understand that the world has been deceived and has a misconception about happiness, let's turn our attention away from world happiness and focus on getting in the mind- set of true happiness. In order to discipline your flesh and nourish your spirit, you must now understand what it means to renew your mind. Most of us have grown up with misconceptions that have contaminated our thinking process. If we never address the misconceptions then we won't change the thought process. For as we think, we are. Our thoughts shape our personality and consequently our behaviors. When we renew our mind, then we can begin to experience that peace, prosperity, and relaxation that defines happiness. Conveniently, this is the topic of the next section. After that, we'll look at some pitfalls to avoid as you walk in the spirit.

II

A New Mind

As we mentioned before, most of our adult thinking has been the cumulative product of worldly ideals. In other words, our thinking has been natural, or carnal, and not spiritual. We have allowed ourselves to adopt what the world considers appropriate and that falls right into Satan's plan. For clarity purposes, I need to speak about demonic influences for a moment. You make choices every day that shape your destiny. If Satan can get you into the habit of making destructive choices, then you will have a destructive life. That's how he destroys you. He can't "make" you do anything. He has to use the weapon of deception to convince you into making those choices. It's like the bad angel (Satan and his demons) on one shoulder and the good angel (the Holy Spirit) on the other. It's not quite set up like that in actuality but it gives you a clear picture of the opposing influences in every Christian's life. Satan plants the seed in the form of a thought, then it is up to us to run with it or not.

Here's the scenario: You've met somebody from your church that you really like and you begin to date. You're still getting to know each other, which usually takes time and effort, so you evaluate every action and reaction hoping to get a sense of what this person is really like. Satan sees an opportunity and he waits for the right time to take advantage. He doesn't want you to be happy; he wants to destroy you. Jesus said, "The thief does not come except to steal and to kill and to destroy. I have come that they may have life, and that they may have it more abundantly." (John 10:10). You're out on a second or third date, and Sally's cell phone rings. She answers the call from her worrying friend Jane who just wants to make sure that she's safe. Jane has a habit of asking a zillion questions; so to avoid the perception of being rude, Sally ends the conversation before Jane can get started. While you're driving, Satan plants the thought: "That must've been someone she doesn't want you to know about because she ended the call so abruptly." You begin to think; "I wonder who that was?" You begin to run with it, "It was probably her old boyfriend checking up on her. They probably talk all the time. After our date, she's probably gonna talk to him and tell him all about it and they'll both have a good laugh. She's not interested in me; she's just passing time. She's probably thinking about him right now." So you turn to Sally and say, "So whatcha thinking about?" Sally thinks this question is a little unusual, so she hesitantly replies, "Nothing." And in your mind, "Nothing?!... *That* confirms it. She's just trying to hide her feelings for him. I can't wait for this date to be over!" Satan has successfully destroyed your evening and possibly your brief relationship with Sally. Now I know this example is somewhat extreme, but it's a very good illustration of what goes on in our heads all the time. Most of the time, we don't even recognize it. How many times have you run with the thoughts that Satan has planted in your mind?

Here's another scenario: You're walking down the street on a beautiful day. Your spirits are high and you feel good. As you pass a stranger you politely say, "Hello," but the stranger just keeps on walking and doesn't even acknowledge you. Satan takes advantage of the opportunity and plants the seed: "That made you look pretty stupid." You run with it: "That stranger wanted to make me look stupid. My friends are always saying that I'm too nice. Well, that all ends now! I'm not speaking to anyone unless they speak to me first!" Satan has successfully stolen your joy for the day and has deceived you into permanently modifying your behavior. The stranger, who was listening to music through his microsized headphones, has no idea of what just happened.

What's truly amazing (and I can't stress this enough) is that this happens all the time, all day long in our minds! It's no wonder so many Christians are living defeated lives. Our thinking has been polluted and it needs to be cleansed. First, we need to identify the enemy. In our scenarios, were Sally and the headphone stranger the enemies? Of course not. In fact, they had no clue about what was going on in your mind. The enemy is the instigator who planted the destructive thoughts in the first place. Satan is the enemy. Therefore our battle is not with other human beings (who at times are also negatively influenced by Satan), but with the spiritual realm of demonic forces. We need to start challenging our thoughts! The next time you start to feel offended, uncomfortable, or defensive, challenge yourself. Ask yourself, "Is this situation my perception of it or do I have enough facts to accurately define it." If you don't have all the facts, then don't allow yourself to run with negative ideas. After Sally hung up her cell phone in our first scenario, why didn't you think, "She's probably planning a surprise for me when we get home, but she doesn't want to spill the beans." You could have assumed any number of positive things, but you chose to run with the destructive one. When we find ourselves running with negative thoughts without having the facts to support our thinking, that's a good indication that we are being destructively influenced by Satan. In our headphone- stranger scenario, why didn't we come to the assumption that the person was preoccupied and genuinely did not hear us? We need to challenge any thinking that makes us uncomfortable and is not in line with the Word of God, Jesus Christ. This is what Paul was talking about in 2 Corinthians 10:3-5 when he said, "For though we walk in the flesh, we do not war according to the flesh. For the weapons of our warfare are not carnal but mighty in God for pulling down strongholds, casting down arguments and every high thing that exalts itself against the knowledge of God, bringing every thought into captivity to the obedience of Christ." The Word tells us that we need to bring every thought into captivity! That's how important your thought life is. Every thought must be weighed against the Word of God. That's how important knowing the Word of God is. This may seem like an impossible challenge but it isn't. We have Christ on our side helping us. And we know we can do all things through Christ. How does Christ help us? By strengthening our thinking with the Word. God already provided the template for happiness in His Word.

Thought Control

You cannot control every situation in your life, but you can control how you react to your situation. Controlling your reactions effectively and consistently can only occur after you've controlled your thoughts. I'm sure you've heard this before:

> Your thoughts become your words, Your words become
> your actions, Your actions become character,
> Your character becomes your destiny.

If you think about this for a moment you understand that it is absolutely true. This clever adage supports Proverbs 23:7, "For as he [a man] thinks in his heart, so is he." Who you are and who you will become are direct results of the thoughts that you've entertained. It's simple cause and effect.

As we started to discuss before, your thought life is controlled by first challenging your thoughts. You may say, "Hey, I don't have time to think about every thought that runs through my mind.

I'll never get anything done because I'll be too busy analyzing all my thoughts." Did you have enough time to develop the habit of letting your thoughts run wild? The bottom line is that you will have to start thinking about what you think about. Once you get into the habit of challenging your thoughts, you'll be doing it regularly without even knowing it.

When should you challenge your thoughts? Whenever your thinking is out of line with the Word of God. As your sensitivity to the Holy Spirit within you develops, you will be made aware of this. It usually begins with a feeling of being uncomfortable. Have you ever caught yourself saying that you just didn't feel good about a decision you made, or a conversation you had? That may have been God's way of letting you know that you we're heading down the wrong track. The Holy Spirit is limitless in the way He communicates with us, but we have to be sensitive to His urging. Let me take a moment to make a couple of points about the Holy Spirit. When we are baptized into the body of Christ, the Holy Spirit indwells us and becomes a part of our lives. "Or do you not know that your body is the temple of the Holy Spirit who is in you, whom you have from God, and you are not your own?" (1 Corinthians 6:19). So what does the Holy Spirit do in us? The Holy Spirit searches our hearts, illuminates our minds, convicts us, comforts us, guides us, and sanctifies us. So getting back to our discussion, the best way to know when to challenge our thoughts is to challenge them when we are urged to challenge them by the Holy Spirit. If your sensitivity to the Holy Spirit is not what you would like it to be, then pray for greater sensitivity. In the meantime, challenge any thought that makes you feel uncomfortable because there is a reason why you feel uncomfortable. What happens after you've challenged your thinking?

Here's the tough part. Once you've challenged your thinking and you've determined that it is not appropriate, make a change! If you're not going to change your thinking, why challenge it in the first place? Making a change for the better is what this is all about. It takes courage to challenge your thinking. It takes determination to make the changes. It takes patience to see it through to the end. Once you start the ball rolling, it will keep rolling. You'll be in a better position to choose happiness. You won't let adverse situations steal your joy. Before you know it, you'll be a different person and people will notice. People will want to be around you because of your pleasant attitude. Your happiness will be contagious. I used to get angry when someone cut in front of me, while I was driving, and then traveled slower than me. This was a big pet peeve of mine. I would make it a point to swerve around them and get back in front. Sometimes I would even slow down just so they'd know how they made me feel. Besides the fact that I could've been shot by someone with road rage, I wasn't able to keep my joy. I would wake up in the morning happy and ready to face the challenges of the day. But I couldn't even make it in to work without that happiness being taken away. Of course I would be a little edgy for the rest of the morning and that would just snowball into other negative things. I had allowed Satan to steal my joy. It's not that he has command over all the cars on the highway, but he had influenced me to believe that the person who cut me off did it on purpose, just to aggravate me. He convinced me that I needed to get even. He convinced me to take it personally and I made the choice to act on what I believed. Then one day, the Holy Spirit helped me to challenge my thinking. As I was discussing my pet peeve with one of my friends, it was brought to my attention that maybe that person who cut me off just saved my life. Maybe they prevented me from being somewhere where an accident was about to occur. Maybe this was God's way of protecting me. Maybe the person in front of me is not a good driver, or has bad eyesight. You get the picture. I realized that I had to challenge that anger. If I had the choice to believe something that made me feel uncomfortable or something that didn't, which one was I going to choose? I may never know why someone cuts me off, but I do know that believing they did it in purpose is unfair, one- sided, and is going to upset me. So I choose not to believe that. If you were to drive with me today, you would never know that I once had a fierce habit of getting upset when someone cuts me off. I react totally different now and I constantly have to make a conscious effort to control my thinking. And it's a lot easier to do now than it was then.

Once you get to the point where you are challenging your thinking, you're on the road to constant joy. We will talk more about constant joy later in the book. Another aspect to changing your thinking is maintaining positive thoughts. If you're regularly thinking positively and challenging the negative thoughts, it's easy to understand why you will develop a cheerful personality. We've talked about challenging your thoughts, now let's discuss spiritual thinking.

Spiritual Thinking

I like to refer to this section as spiritual thinking instead of positive thinking because positive thinking works in conjunction with spiritual thinking. Positive thinking focuses on eliminating negative thoughts and substituting them with positive ones, thus exercising control of your thought life. Spiritual thinking focuses on attacking your demons by using the Word as your sword. If positive thinking can be viewed as our defense, then spiritual thinking is our offense. Our defense stops Satan from advancing on our joy. Our offense is what allows us to advance through Satan's defenses and enjoy God's blessings of the Spirit. Whether you see them as offense or defense, they are both very important for victory over Satan. Satan's job is ultimately to steal from us, kill us, and destroy us. He wants to rob us of every good thing God has in store for us. Satan has been ruining things for us from the beginning in the Garden of Eden. If he attacked Adam and Eve and their descendants, including Christ, then he obviously will come after us. We're all vulnerable, but when we stand in Christ, all things are possible.

Let's see what the Bible has to say about the word of God. "For the word of God is living and powerful, and sharper than any two-edged sword, piercing even to the division of soul and spirit, and of joints and marrow, and is a discerner of the thoughts and intents of the heart. And there is no creature hidden from His sight, but all things are naked and open to the eyes of Him to whom we must give account." (Hebrews 4:12- 13). This is the weapon God intended for us to use against Satan. What a powerful weapon! The key here is that our sword is alive and there's nothing it can't cut! Why should you be afraid of any creature with this sword in your hand? Do you notice how active our quest for happiness has become? We are actually at war. Whether you want to be at war or not, Satan is going to attack you. If you choose God, His yoke is easy and His burden is light. The battle is actually His. You are either for God or against God. Your job is to obey His instructions. God's Word is full of instructions. If you don't know these instructions, it will make things more confusing for you. Get into the Word, you're life depends on it! God even gives us instructions about how to dress for this spiritual warfare in Ephesians 6:13-17, "Therefore take up the whole armor of God, that you may be able to withstand in the evil day, and having done all, to stand. Stand therefore, having girded your waist with truth, having put on the breastplate of righteousness, and having shod your feet with the preparation of the gospel of peace; above all, taking the shield of faith with which you will be able to quench all the fiery darts of the wicked one. And take the helmet of salvation, and the sword of the Spirit, which is the word of God." Our weapons are truth, righteousness, peace, faith, salvation, and the Word of God. Jesus said, "I am the way, the truth, and the life. No one comes to the Father except through Me." (John 14:6). The truth sustains you and keeps you in position. In Ephesians 6:13-17, I think of the truth as a belt that keeps your pants from falling down. If you've ever been caught in a lie, then you know it feels like you're standing in the middle of a crowd with you're pants down. You're in no position to fight with your pants down so stay in the truth.

Righteousness is where God has placed you. It means, as Christians, you have rights. It means you have been placed in good standing with God and sin can no longer separate you from God because you are dead to sin and risen with Christ. You did not deserve to be placed in this position and receive God's grace (unmerited favor). You are the righteousness of God because you have believed in Him, not because of anything you accomplished. John 3:16-18 says, "For God so loved the world that He gave His only begotten Son, that whoever believes in Him should not perish but have everlasting life. For God did not send His Son into the world to condemn the world, but that the world through Him might be saved. He who believes in Him is not condemned; but he who does not believe is condemned already, because he has not believed in the name of the only begotten Son of God." This should bring you confidence. You can stick out your chest because your righteousness has got you covered.

Peace is one of the fruits of the Spirit. Peace makes us ready to deal with any situation. When we act from a position of peace, we give ourselves the best chance for success. There is power in peace that gives us an advantage over the enemy. You automatically become a better decision maker when you make decisions from a position of peace. So be at peace knowing that God is on your side and victory has already been assured because God is love and love never fails.

Faith in Jesus will shield you from doubts and fears. When

you make a mistake and Satan tries to weaken you with guilt, your faith in Psalm 103:12 will help you to stand strong. When your confidence is fading and you don't believe that you can carry on, your faith in Philippians 4:13 will build you up again. When you fear a surprise attack from the enemy or you can't seem to find your way, your faith in Psalm 91:11-12 will make you feel secure. When you're frustrated because you feel like you've messed up too many times to be given another chance, your faith in Psalm 136 will illuminate your thinking. When you feel like you've fallen too far off the path and you feel that you are unreachable, your faith in Romans 8:38-39 will comfort you. When you can't seem to stop worrying about little things, your faith in Matthew 6:25-26 will keep you calm. When you feel unworthy of God's love for whatever reason, your faith in John 3:16-18 will elevate your self-worth. Your faith in Jesus is your shield from the fiery darts of guilt, fear, doubts, worrying, and frustration that the enemy will throw at you.

Salvation is our victory over death, for the gift of God is eternal life. God said in Hosea 13:14, "I will ransom them from the power of the grave; I will redeem them from death. O Death, I will be your plagues! O Grave, I will be your destruction! Pity is hidden from My eyes." That's what God has to say to Death and Destruction on our behalf. Knowing that you are saved puts you in a position where you don't fear death. You can act without fear of dying! Praise God!

And most importantly, you have a sword that is alive and there's nothing it can't cut! *There is nothing it can't cut.* Our weapons are truth, righteousness, peace, faith, salvation, and the word of God. Truly we are more than prepared for victory over the enemy.

Spiritual thinking involves getting into the Word. Victory is already assured and no weapon that the enemy can devise shall prosper against us because God says so. God has already done His part to assure victory for us. We need to accept Him and do our part. What's our part? After we have accepted Jesus as our personal Savior, then we need to walk with Him. This means we need to consider our ways and alter our behavior so that it is in line with what God expects from us. (Pop Quiz: Where do we find out what God expects from us?) Yeah, I hate pop quizzes, too, but this was an easy one. Now that we know what we need to do to control our thoughts and awaken our spiritual thinking, we need to focus on eliminating the negative thinking. The next section discusses the negative effects complaining can have on your happiness and how to avoid it altogether.

Stop Complaining

One of the quickest ways to turn your thinking from positive to negative is to start complaining. If you pay attention, you can actually feel your mood start to swing. When you feel yourself starting to get into complain mode you have given yourself over to the enemy who throws fiery darts at you. Remember that the enemy's purpose in throwing those darts is to kill and destroy. You get hit with a negative thought dart and then you start complaining. Satan and his demons begin to rejoice because they have achieved success. They know that if you complain long enough and passionately enough, you will lose your joy and you may even do something negative, which would be icing on the cake for them. Remember that your thoughts become your actions. So if they can foul up your thought life, they can foul up your behavior. It all starts in the mind. This doesn't mean that you can never discuss your situation with someone, or get a heavy load off your chest, or explore different options. It means that you need to be careful. Be careful to discuss your situation with someone that's positive, preferably a Christian. The enemy attacks everyone, even your friends. It's important to realize that sometimes your friends can be the ones that Satan is using to inject the negative thoughts into your world. Ultimately you have to make the right decisions for yourself. You have to decide what thoughts to entertain or not.

Another opportunity that the enemy uses is negative situations. When bad things happen, we instinctively complain. It's as if the complaining is therapeutic. Some of us reason that by cussing and fussing we are actually avoiding doing something negative. Sometimes we just feel like we *have* to complain in order to let people know how we feel. The truth is that nothing good comes from complaining. It's a doorway for the enemy to get in our heads. For those of you who may still find this hard to believe, I encourage you to read the book of Job in the Bible. Job would not curse God even when he lost all his wealth. Joseph found favor in God's eyes and showed his brothers love even though they sold him as a slave. And Jesus didn't complain when He was being nailed to the cross for *our* sins. You may be saying to yourself, "But, Brian, these were special men. You can't possibly expect me to live like Jesus." I'm not expecting you to live like Jesus, God is. The Bible says in 1 John 4:15 (New International Version), "If anyone acknowledges that Jesus is the Son of God, God lives in him and he in God." First John 2:6 (NIV) says, "Whoever claims to live in him must walk as Jesus did." We should take comfort knowing that we have enough power in Jesus to stop complaining and that we can do all things through Christ.

What about venting? If I'm actually venting, then isn't that a good thing? No. It is good to have someone to be an ear for you, especially someone in Christ. It is good to have someone you can discuss personal issues with, but ultimately it is God who provides the answers. We should seek God first through prayer before we seek advice from a friend, counselor, pastor, deacon, etc. Sometimes God uses the people closest to us to help guide us through difficult times. Sometimes God uses complete strangers. God works in mysterious ways. We have to trust in Him to give us comfort, direction, and deliverance. We may not understand why we are going through what we are going through, but God is always in control. You are exactly where you are supposed to be right now—this year, this month, this minute. You're reading this book for a reason. God is molding you into the person He wants you to be. When you truly understand that, you will welcome change and challenges, because you will know that your circumstances are only temporary. When you overcome one situation, you will have become a stronger, better person for the next. Understanding combats anger and frustration. Anger and frustration create a need for venting. So, as you develop your understanding, you combat the need to vent. Here's what Proverbs, generally regarded as the book of wisdom, has to say about understanding:

> Proverbs 11:12 (NIV)
>
> A man who lacks judgment derides his neighbor, but a man of understanding holds his tongue.
>
> Proverbs 14:29 (NIV)
>
> A patient man has great understanding, but a quick-tempered man displays folly.
>
> Proverbs 17:27 (NIV)
>
> A man of knowledge uses words with restraint, and a man of understanding is even tempered.
>
> Proverbs 18:2 (NIV)
>
> A fool finds no pleasure in understanding but delights in airing his own opinions.

These few passages helped me to appreciate the value of understanding early in life. When I was in high school, my father suggested that I read one Bible verse a day. Being that I was in Catholic schools from grades 1-12, this wasn't a hard thing to do. One of the first books of the Bible I read was Proverbs. It's a good book to read if you're just starting out, and it's a good refresher for those who may have read it before. Some of you may be asking, "Well, if understanding is so important, how do I get it?" This is a good question, especially considering that Proverbs also suggest that we lean not on our own understanding. Now before you go saying that the Bible is contradicting itself let's review a few things. Man is a triune being. He is spirit, soul, and body. The soul consists of the mind, will, and emotions. A man's natural, carnal understanding develops in his mind. Man is also a spiritual being. His spiritual understanding is developed by the Word of God. So when Proverbs 3:5 says, "Trust in the Lord with all your heart and lean not on your own understanding," this means that you should not trust in your natural, carnal understanding but in the Lord. The more you read and learn about God, the easier it will be to trust Him. This brings us back to our original question: How do we gain understanding? By expanding our knowledge of the Word. "But, Brian, getting to know the Word is your answer to everything!" You're right, it is...you'll see. Some of us complain because we use it to get what we want. It becomes a manipulative tool. We complain because we figure either someone will feel sorry for us and give us what we want out of pity or people will just get tired of hearing us and give us what we want to quiet us. Either way, it's manipulative. The dictionary defines "manipulate" *as, "to handle, manage, or use, especially with skill, in some process of treatment or performance."* When we manipulate a situation, we are skillfully handling and managing that situation. In other words, we are taking that situation into our own hands. We need to realize that God is in control. We shouldn't be manipulating people to get what we want. We should be asking God to provide for us and to meet all our needs. We shouldn't be taking situations into our own hands. We need to let go and let God. James 4:2 says, "You lust and do not have. You murder and covet and cannot obtain. You fight and war. Yet you do not have because you do not ask." Romans 8:32 says, "He who did not spare His own Son, but delivered Him up for us all, how shall He not with Him also freely give us all things?" The next time we feel the need to manipulate someone to get what we what, we should immediately go to a private place and cast all of our concerns, desires, and needs on God through earnest, faithful prayer. In fact, that's exactly what He wants us to do. He wants to be our Savior, our rock, and our provider. He loves us! Whether we complain because we believe it's therapeutic, we feel a need to vent, or we're just being manipulative, we need to stop because nothing good comes from it. We need to learn from the examples that Joseph, Job, and Jesus left for us. These men had plenty of reason to complain, yet they put their trust in Father God when times got tough. Complaining opens doorways for Satan to steal our joy. It also turns us away from understanding and it can cause us to take situations into our own hands. Let's walk in love, heeding these next two verses: "And do not grumble, as some of them did—and were killed by the destroying angel." (1 Corinthians 10:10 NIV). "Do everything without complaining or arguing." (Philippians 2:14 NIV).

Walking in the Spirit

Once we get to the point where we can identify negative thinking and start thinking positively or spiritually, we can begin to move in the direction where we can walk in the Spirit of love. Romans 12:2 says, "And do not be conformed to this world, but be transformed by the renewing of your mind, that you may prove what is that good and acceptable and perfect will of God." Our thinking actually transforms us. The word "renew" is significant here because it illustrates the fact that we are ever changing and that we influence our circumstance all the time. In other words, it's not good enough to go to church on Sunday and get your thinking renewed with some powerful preaching. We have to continuously keep our minds set on spiritual principles outlined for us in the Bible because Satan is constantly trying to pollute our thinking everyday of the week. Initially it will take some effort on our part, but eventually it will be as natural as breathing. As we let the Holy Spirit work in us, we will be led into the spiritual path. The Spirit of God is gentle and patient. The Spirit of God would never make us do anything against our will. After all, it was God who gave us free will. God wants our will to be in line with His. He wants us to realize that He is in control and He will look out for our best interest better than we can for ourselves. Jesus describes it this way, "I am the vine, you are the branches. He who abides in Me, and I in him, bears much fruit; for without Me you can do nothing." (John 15:5). So how will you know that you are walking in the Spirit? When you bear much fruit. What kind of fruit? Spiritual fruit, which is the fruit of the Spirit of God. "But the fruit of the Spirit is love, joy, peace, long-suffering, kindness, goodness, faithfulness, gentleness, self-control. Against such there is no law." (Galatians 5:22-23).

Spiritual Fruit

By examining the concept of spiritual fruit, we can better understand what it means to walk in the Spirit. If we look at Galatians 5:22-23 in conjunction with John 15:5, we can safely come to the following conclusion. When we see someone whose life is characterized by love, joy, peace, long-suffering, kindness, goodness, faithfulness, gentleness, and self- control, we know that Jesus lives in that person and is responsible for those characteristics. If Jesus did not live in that person, then we would not see those characteristics because the only way that person could produce all those characteristics is through Jesus. Let's examine the fruit of the Spirit.

Love

Love is the first spiritual fruit mentioned in Galatians 5:22-23. God is love. Love is the most powerful force in the universe. It's what causes us to move in the direction of God. Many songs, movies, and novels have been centered on love. Love is the common thread between Christians. Matthew 22:37-39 puts it in perspective for us. Jesus says, "You shall love the Lord your God with all your heart, with all your soul, and with all your mind. This is the first and greatest commandment. And the second is like it: You shall love your neighbor as yourself." All of the commandments and laws in the Bible are based on love. It's because God loved us that He gave us His Word in the first place. "OK Brian, I see the importance of love, but what are the characteristics of love? How do I know I'm loving correctly when there's so many definitions of love?" Love is not properly defined in love songs; it's not always properly depicted in the movies, and some of the best novels don't even get it right. Considering the amount of music we listen to, movies we go and see, and novels we read, it's easy to see why there's so much confusion about what love is. The truth about love is laid out explicitly in 1 Corinthians 13. Most Christians have probably heard excerpts from this chapter at weddings. The apostle Paul masterfully describes love in such a way that it has been referenced over the years as the definition of love itself. Carefully read this chapter of the Bible and remove any confusion about what love is.

> *If I speak in the tongues of men and of angels, but have not love, I am only a resounding gong or a clanging cymbal. If I have the gift of prophecy, and can fathom all mysteries and all knowledge, and if I have faith, that can move mountains, but have not love, I am nothing. If I give all I possess to the poor, and surrender my body to the flames, but have not love, I gain*

nothing. Love is patient, love is kind. It does not envy; it does not boast, it is not proud. It is not rude, it is not self-seeking, it is not easily angered, it keeps no record of wrongs. Love does not delight in evil but rejoices in the truth. It always protects, always trust, always hopes, always perseveres. Love never fails. But where there are prophecies, they will cease; where there are tongues, they will be stilled; where there is knowledge, it will pass away. For we know in part and we prophesy in part. But when perfection comes, the imperfect disappears. When I was a child, I talked like a child, I thought like a child, I reasoned like a child. When I became a man, I put childish ways behind me. Now we see a poor reflection as in a mirror, then we shall see face to face. Now I know in part; then I shall know fully, even as I am fully known. And now these three remain: faith, hope, and love. But the greatest of these is love.

Joy

The spiritual fruit of joy is a power that goes unused by most Christians. Yes, joy is a power. It keeps us steadfast in faith. It battles fatigue, depression, and all negativity. It sustains us and is emotionally refreshing. If we stay focused on the promises of God, we can acquire and maintain joy, which provides us with strength and peace. If someone told you that you won the fifty-million-dollar lottery, would it bother you knowing that you were thousands of dollars in debt? Would it bother you that your car was falling apart or that you didn't have new clothes? Of course it wouldn't. You're a millionaire. Although you hadn't cashed in your lottery ticket and although you hadn't seen any of the money, you'd be filled with joy because you'd know that you had millions of dollars to address all of those issues, wouldn't you? That's how excited we all should be about the promises of God. Although our sin debt is outrageous, Psalm 103:12 says,

"As far as the east is from the west, so far has He removed our transgressions from us." Although our world may be falling apart all around us, Psalm 91:11-12 says, "For He shall give his angels charge over you, to keep you in all your ways. They shall bear you up in their hands, lest you dash your foot against a stone." And although we've never physically seen God and sometimes question whether He's still with us, Deuteronomy 31:6 says, "Be strong and of good courage, do not fear nor be afraid of them; for the Lord your God, He is the One who goes with you. He will not leave you nor forsake you." We have every reason to be joyful and full of confidence in God's Word. In fact, it is that same confidence that allows us to have peace.

Peace

"You will keep in perfect peace him whose mind is steadfast, because he trust in you." (Isaiah 26:3). How do we attain peace? By keeping our minds on the promises of God and trusting Him completely. We will have "perfect" peace by doing this. The power of peace is incredible. We've talked about peace briefly in the first section. Peace is the beginning of happiness. If you don't have peace in your life, you will continue to be anxious, stressed-out, and full of worries. How can you be happy under those circumstances? Isaiah 26:3 also reveals that God keeps those who trust in Him, in perfect peace. In other words, God makes Himself responsible for your peace when you trust in Him and stay focused on Him. This is also reinforced by Jesus in John 14:27, "Peace I leave with you, My peace I give to you; not as the world gives do I give to you. Let not your hearts be troubled, neither let it be afraid." So we see that when we obey God, He is responsible for our perfect peace. Jesus says that He doesn't give as the world gives. How does the world give? When I was a child, my Aunt Audrey told me that nothing in this world is free. She said that when someone offers you something and they say it's free, it's because they want something from you. With all of my infinite wisdom at fourteen years old, I had a hard time believing that. We were driving in the car on our way back from a weekend at her house in Chicago and I became determined to prove her wrong. I said, "Look there. The sign says Buy One and Get One Free." My aunt said, "If it was really free, you wouldn't have to buy one at the regular price first." I said, "Look there, the sign says Free Car Wash." She said, "It's free when you purchase at least eight gallons of gas." We went on and on for about ten minutes and finally it dawned on me that she was right. When the world gives you something, it's really a deceptive tactic used to take from you. The devil is crafty and he is the father of lies. See what happens when you sign up for a free credit card in the mail. See what happens when you accept a free gift for your signature. See what happens when you sign up for a free service. A free credit card usually means giving someone access to your credit report. This information can be manipulated and sold. Giving away your signature opens the doorway for many evils. I once signed my signature on a comment card for a free hat or something and they took my signature and switched my long distance provider. When you sign up for a free service, it's usually free for the first month. This is how the world gives. Jesus gives freely, meaning that He gives without deceit and without trying to sneak something out of you. Jesus does expect something from you when He gives and He does want to take from you when He gives. The difference is, He's not deceitful or sneaky about it. Jesus expects you to trust in Him so that He can give you deliverance and He wants to take away your hatred, grief, and discomfort when He gives you love, joy, and peace. Seems too easy, doesn't it? Well, according to Jesus, it is easy. Jesus says in Matthew 11:28-30, "Come to Me, all you who labor and are heavy laden, and I will give you rest. Take My yoke upon you and learn from Me, for I am gentle and lowly in heart, and you will find rest for your souls. For My yoke is easy and My burden is light." No matter what our circumstances, we should trust in God. Even when it gets rough and we have to suffer through certain situations, we know that God is in control and we will be stronger in the end. Jesus is the way to peace.

Long-Suffering

Long-suffering is the fire by which we are all proven. Sometimes we have to go through certain things until weakness is overcome. Long- suffering is also described as patience or endurance. All three words are actually connected to each other. For by suffering or enduring through a situation, we develop our patience. Endurance requires patience and patience allows us to endure through our suffering. Suffering long brings out all that's in your heart, just like fire burns all that which is flammable. We are put to the fire every day so that in the end we shall come forth as pure gold. All of the impurities will have been burned off. It is God who purifies us and long- suffering is part of the purification process. All questions will be answered through the purification process. What types of questions? Will you tithe faithfully even when your finances are strained? Will you love your enemy when your enemy spitefully uses you? Will you turn your cares over to God and refuse to worry about your situation even though you don't understand what's going on? Some of these questions take a lifetime to answer, and there are many questions. This is why we are to show patience and endure through each situation, knowing that Jesus is with us and that we will not fail. Jesus will never leave us and He is our power and strength. Jesus is love and love never fails. We can do all things through Christ. So we see that long-suffering is a gift from God that we should accept with understanding because we know that as we suffer, we are being purified. The apostle Peter puts it this way, "Beloved, do not think it strange concerning the fiery trial which is to try you, as though some strange thing happened to you; but rejoice to the extent that you partake of Christ's sufferings, that when His glory is revealed, you may also be glad with exceeding joy." (1 Peter 4:12-13). Because we suffer with Christ, we shall also partake of His glory. Your endurance may also be an inspiration to others, so let your perseverance build as you patiently endure your trials and tribulations.

Kindness

Kindness seems easy enough to understand, right? I mean, Christians should be kind people. This simple principle, however, can be difficult to perform. Christians aren't called to be kind only to other Christians, but we are called to be kind to all people—even our enemies. Jesus says in Luke 6:35, "But love your enemies, do good, and lend, hoping for nothing in return; and your reward will be great, and you will be sons of the Highest. For He is kind to the unthankful and evil." So we see that God rewards us for doing good to others. I was in the grocery store a few months ago, and I had an opportunity to put kindness (and meekness) into action. An older man and I were approaching the cashier at the same time from different directions. The man had about ten items in his shopping cart and I had two items in my hand. Clearly, I was closer to the cashier by a few seconds than he was, but I didn't want to race to the cashier, and I was hoping he would usher me ahead being that I only had two items in my hand. So I walked casually to the cashier, and we ended up meeting at the same time. He almost ran me over with his cart, trying to beat me to the cashier. I saw this as an opportunity to be kind. I just smiled and got in back of him. Now you may be saying, "How is that being kind?" I was being kind by allowing him to have his way and not getting angry about it. I was being unselfish. I could've made a stink about it and got my way, but sometimes it takes meekness in order to be kind. Sometimes we mistake kindness for weakness, but it actually took strength for me not to make an issue out of the situation. Well, as he was unloading his cart, he dropped his container of berries, and they spilled all over the place. The cashier called for someone to clean it up and made him wait until the mess at the register was cleaned. In the meantime, the same cashier moved to another register and motioned for me to come over. As she checked me out, I couldn't help but think that in his haste, he brought that mess upon himself. I didn't take pleasure in his misfortune, but I feel that God rewarded me with fairness for being kind.

Goodness

Goodness and kindness are similar and it's difficult to separate them. One distinction is that goodness is the opposite of evilness. In this way, goodness is also a synonym for godliness. This leads me to define "goodness" as that which is derived from pure love. What you do out of love is what I would consider goodness. This is why it is important to have love in your heart. The more love you have in your heart, the more ready and willing you will be to do that which is good. This is why we pray for Jesus to come into our hearts. Jesus can purge our black hearts and fill them with love. When that happens, kindness can be shown out of the goodness in your heart.

Faithfulness

We naturally associate faithfulness with loyalty. We can all relate to a faithful dog or a faithful friend or a faithful spouse. But faithfulness is more than loyalty. Faithfulness is a spiritual fruit that is authored by God. Spiritually speaking, "faithfulness" means the degree to which one is full of faith. "Faith" is defined in Hebrews 11:1 as "The substance of things hoped for, the evidence of things not seen." Faith is a force that we can use to draw the power of God. Faith works in the spiritual realm, much the same way gravity works in the natural world. When we apply the force of faith to a situation, we begin to attract, pull, and coerce things in the spiritual world so that our circumstances in the natural world develop according to our faith. Jesus explains why his disciples were unable to cast out demons in Matthew 17:20 (NIV). "Because you have so little faith. I tell you the truth, if you have faith as small as a mustard seed, you can say to this mountain, 'Move from here to there' and it will move. Nothing will be impossible for you." All we have to do is believe in the power of God. We don't have to have all the answers, we just have to have faith. When our situations seem impossible, we should be all the more faithful. When we are full of faith, nothing is impossible. How do we get faith? Paul says in Romans 10:17, "So then faith comes by hearing, and hearing by the word of God." As we meditate in the Word of God, we increase our faith. God wants us to put our faith in Him. Salvation itself is attained through faith. Paul says in Romans 10:9, "That if you confess with your mouth the Lord Jesus and believe in your heart that God has raised Him from the dead, you will be saved." God wants us to choose life and be saved. This is why we can't begin to please God without faith. Start increasing your faith today. Pray for vision. Ask God to open your spiritual eyes and reveal those things that have been hindering your relationship with Christ. When you pray, believe that God heard you and will answer your prayers. Finish your prayer "in the name of Jesus" and I promise God will reveal something to you that you weren't even aware of.

Gentleness

This is very important. We as Christians need to do a better job of utilizing the spiritual fruit of gentleness. God is gentle. He does not force Himself on us. Instead He gives us free will. He does not punish us for our transgressions. Instead He forgives our sins when we repent. He does not explode in anger although we continue to do things that are unpleasing to Him. Instead His mercy endures forever and He gives us another chance to get it right. Unfortunately we sometimes stifle the spirit of gentleness inside of us for a variety of different reasons. We have to get it right. We don't have the right to mistreat others just because they have mistreated us. God forgives us our trespasses the way we forgive those who trespass against us. We should be gentle with each other at all times, especially when others are not being gentle with us. This can be very difficult to do, especially when we've been conditioned to "get even" with those who wrong us. I've struggled with this throughout my life, and I continuously have to keep myself in check. When someone wrongs me, especially a loved one, I remind myself that vengeance doesn't belong to me. It belongs to God, and He will make right the wrongdoings better than I ever could. I tell myself that God is watching me, and He takes pleasure when I sacrifice my reputation and my desires to get even so that He can get the glory as I put my trust in Him. Like many kids, I was bullied in school. Also, my mother died of cancer when I was five, and I grew up with two different stepmothers. There were many times in my childhood when I was mistreated, and I carried those feelings of resentment and mistrust into my adult life. Of course I didn't realize it at the time, but in my early twenties, I discovered that I didn't trust women, and I was ready to get physical with anyone whom I suspected of disrespecting me. I was far from gentle and I believed that it was just a matter of time before I found myself in serious fisticuffs. I was very familiar with the Bible because I had read it from time to time consistently. Even in those years when I didn't have a church home, I would read my Bible for my personal development. The problem was that I wasn't applying all the principles that I was learning. As I applied the Word of God to my life, my circumstances would change. As I began to trust God for my protection, I began to depend less on myself and more on God. Before, I would go out of my way to deny anyone of the pleasure of disrespecting me. In time, I would learn to let go and let God. I became less defensive and more dependent on God. It became clear to me that it wasn't as important to mistrust women as it was to totally trust in God. I learned to believe that if someone was hiding something from me, God would shine light on it and reveal it to me. As I came to see it, I would know what I'm supposed to know. After all, God knows everything and He's in my corner. I haven't had a serious fistfight in over a decade. I'm far from perfect, but I know that victory is mine. When God gets through with me, I shall come forth as pure gold. The point is that being gentle is important because it is God-like, and we should be God-like because we're children of God. I'm gentler than I've ever been although I still have a long way to go.

Self-Control

Who hasn't struggled with self-control? Spiritual self- control refers to the battle between flesh and spirit that we all go through every day. We have to control our fleshy desires. We have to control our appetites, our lusts, and our cravings, otherwise they will control us. If we live a hedonistic life, our spiritual growth will be stifled. The flesh battles the spirit. It is its polar opposite, which is why it must be controlled. We cannot serve two masters. Either we will serve the flesh or the Spirit. Our charge as Christians is to develop spiritually and control our flesh. Without spiritual endowment, we don't have the power to control the flesh. This is why God gives us the spiritual fruit of self-control to aid us in our struggle. Controlling the flesh takes dedication and commitment. The flesh craves after things of the flesh, and the spirit craves after things of the spirit. What we feed we will cause to grow. When we feed our flesh by giving in to its desires, it grows. As it grows, it begins to take control of our lives. The same is true for the spirit. Again, we see how God has given us a choice. We can feed our flesh or feed our spirit. As the spirit grows, the fruits of the spirit multiply. The spiritual fruit of self-control grows stronger as we feed our spirit. How do we feed our spirit? Through prayer, fasting, speaking in tongues, Bible study, worship, meditation on the Word, and fellowshipping with other Christians. These are just some of the ways we can nurture and strengthen our spirit. It takes time to develop your spirit in such a way that it has control over your flesh. Think about this way; you've probably been feeding your flesh most of your life. If that's true, your flesh probably has a stronghold (a fortress) in your life. You have to constantly increase and train your spiritual army so that it can be strong enough to overthrow the fortress of the flesh. The fortress of the flesh is made up of ten thousand strong men with veteran officers and keen fighters. If you've recently began your journey towards spiritual growth, then your spiritual army is made up of one thousand strong men who are still learning the techniques to outwit the army of the flesh. The army of the flesh has dominated the army of the spirit for years. It has a fortress that is well established. Here's the dynamics: When you give in to your flesh, your flesh army grows. When you nurture your spirit, your spiritual army grows. In that sense, you are in control.

So nurture your spirit. **Love** and trust in God, and He will bring you **peace**. Never cease to display **kindness** and **goodness**, for it will bring joy to your spirit. Your **faithfulness** in God's Word will bring you through your **long-suffering**. And as the Spirit of God indwells your spirit, you will display **gentleness** and **self-control** in all that you do.

III

Forgive—You Can't Afford Not To

No relationship can survive without forgiveness. We are human and we make mistakes. Sometimes our mistakes hurt people's feelings. And then there's the choice: Will we hold on to that hurt or let it go? Will we try to get even or will we let God fight our battles? It all comes down to the choice we make. When we hold on to hurt and pain, we continue to hurt and have pain. When we let go of hurt and pain, we no longer hurt and have pain. Although the principle is childishly simple, it can be extremely difficult to perform. We have problems with forgiveness not because we don't understand it, but because it's a spiritual concept that works against our flesh. When we forgive, we have overridden our natural desire to retaliate. We can't allow our carnal instincts to dominate our actions. We simply can't afford to.

The Problem

If there were no transgressions, there wouldn't be a need to forgive. But because of transgressions, or sins, the need for forgiveness is real. As long as we are in this human form, we will struggle with sin. Our flesh seeks after things of the flesh. It wants to be pleased, and it doesn't care at what costs. In fact, the fruit of the flesh is the exact opposite of fruit of the spirit. Meaning that if you are living with hate, strife, harshness, corruption, sorrow, doubt, or hedonism, you are operating in the flesh. These are the types of things that accompany the flesh. If we allow the flesh to have its way, it will obviously destroy us. You may be living with only a few of these things, but don't be fooled. Satan wants you to believe that you can get by with operating in only a few of these areas. You can't. The truth is that your flesh doesn't just seek after one or two of these things, it seeks after all things that are of the flesh. Also, if your flesh has already weakened you in one area, then it will try to continue to weaken you in that area until the day you die. How many people do you know that started out smoking two cigarettes per day, and two years later they still smoke only two cigarettes per day? Not many. And during those two years, what other fleshy desires have they succumbed to? How long can you carry hatred before it turns into strife? How long can you carry sorrow and doubt before it turns into depression? If you're operating in the flesh, it's only a matter of time before it destroys you. When you operate in the flesh you're not only hurting yourself, you're hurting others. You are in pain and you can't see the big picture. What you can't see is the eternal price you're paying by operating in the flesh.

The Price

Operating in the flesh is operating in sin. The flesh works against the Spirit. And Paul tells us in Romans 6:23, "For the wages of sin is death." In other words, the price you ultimately pay for operating in the flesh is death. Not just physical death; we all expect to die whether we are holy or unholy. The death Paul refers to here is the condemnation of the soul, which is eternal death. You don't have to be an accountant, investor, or financial analyst to realize that operating in the flesh isn't worth eternal condemnation, right? You may be tallying up the physical pain and suffering that comes with denying yourself of fleshy pleasures. You may be trying to compare that with what God has in store for us after we die to see if it's worth it. Paul says in Romans 8:18, "For I consider that the sufferings of this present time are not worthy to be compared with the glory which shall be revealed in us." In addition to an eternal price, there's a price we pay while our physical bodies are still alive. When we operate in the flesh, we are destroying our spirit, which means that we can't have victory here on earth. That's right, as Christians we are supposed to be living in victory. We are supposed to be living Spirit- led lives as we operate in love while being guided by the Word of God. This produces victory for us now. We are to be more than conquerors now because God wants it that way. But we can't be conquerors while we operate in the flesh because it is through our spirit that we obtain victory. And as we operate in the flesh, we stifle our spirit. So by operating in the flesh, we pay a stifling price now and an eternal price later. Put simply, it just ain't worth it.

The Solution

God has masterfully provided the solution, which is forgiveness. "Blessed is he whose transgression is forgiven, whose sin is covered. Blessed is the man to whom the Lord does not impute iniquity." (Psalm 32:1- 2). Jesus paid the price for our sins on the cross. When we acknowledge and repent our sins to God, he is faithful to forgive us and cleanse us from all unrighteousness. Without God's forgiveness we would be damned, for the wages of sin is death. But thanks to Jesus, we have been justified. "There is therefore now no condemnation to those who are in Christ Jesus, who do not walk according to the flesh, but according to the Spirit. For the law of the Spirit of life in Christ Jesus has made me free from the law of sin and death." (Romans 8:1-2). Because of Jesus, we are reconciled to the Father. God sent His own Son to be a living sacrifice for our sins so that we would not perish. That's how much He loves us! What a merciful God we serve! God has provided the solution, and all we have to do is receive it.

We have the power to receive God's forgiveness and the power to block God's forgiveness. Jesus says in Matthew 6:14-15, "For if you forgive men their trespasses, your heavenly Father will also forgive you. But if you do not forgive men their trespasses, neither will your Father forgive your trespasses." In order to keep the gates of God's mercy open, we have to keep our gates of mercy open. So again we have a choice. God has revealed it all very plainly. We must forgive others for our own sakes. Just as God operated in love to provide a way for us to be reconciled to Him, we must operate in love and provide a way to be reconciled to those who have wronged us. Forgiveness is a shackle-breaking spiritual force. We have been deceived into thinking that we are somehow hurting those who wrong us by not forgiving them. The truth is that we are only hurting ourselves. We are destroying ourselves spiritually and physiologically. Spiritually we are closing the gates of God's mercy, which can hurt us a number of ways. When we are operating in unforgiveness, or "carrying a grudge," we can't receive God's healing, our prayers are not as effective, and we can't prosper spiritually—not to mention that we aren't being forgiven for our trespasses. Carrying a grudge also hurts us physiologically. We have trouble forming new relationships when we're carrying a grudge. Have you ever tried to develop a new relationship with someone who was still carrying a grudge from a previous relationship? It's a difficult situation. Carrying a grudge also opens the doorway to hatred, animosity, strife, and depression. These are all unhealthy feelings, which have been shown to weaken our immune system. So, in addition to keeping God's mercy flowing in our direction, forgiveness also strengthens our spirit and helps to keep us healthy. There is just no way to justify paying the price of being unforgiving. I believe fear is one of the main reasons we don't practice forgiveness the way we should. We're afraid people will walk all over us if we continue to forgive them for hurting us. We're afraid people will think we're pushovers and not respect us. We're afraid people will make fun of us and ridicule us because they think we're weak. But we can't be concerned about our reputation with men and women, we have to be concerned with our reputation with God. And God wants us to forgive constantly. In Luke 17:3, Jesus says to His disciples, "Take heed to yourselves. If your brother sins against you, rebuke him; and if he repents forgive him. And if he sins against you seven times in a day, and seven times in a day returns to you saying, 'I repent,' you shall forgive him." The beautiful thing is that God forgives us the same way. Seven times a day sounds like a lot when someone is sinning against us, but when we're talking about our sins, seven doesn't sound like a large number at all, does it? We have to stop allowing fear of embarrassment, fear of vulnerability, and fear of rejection to hold us back from being forgiving. Fear is a major weapon that the enemy uses against us. Let's talk about fear.

IV

Overcoming Fear

Fear is simply the result of uncontrolled thoughts. If you don't control the thoughts that Satan plants in your mind, you will be led into fear, sadness, depression, and all sorts of unclean, unhealthy, and inappropriate situations. Fear and deception are the enemy's main weapons against you. But again, it's important to be clear. We decide whether to believe, or come into agreement with the thoughts. Satan's power is actually very limited when you think about it. He can only plant thoughts. He can't make you fear, make you sad, or deceive you until you agree with what he has planted in your mind. That's why the Word instructs us to bring into captivity every thought, argument, or idea that goes against the Word of God (see 2 Corinthians 10:5-6). If we control our thoughts, we can remain in the Spirit and in God's rest, or sacred place of refuge. It's all about winning the battle of our minds. Satan wants our souls (our mind, will, and emotions). But he can't have our souls if we give our souls to Christ. That means that we have to renew our mind through the Word so that our will can be in agreement with God's will and our emotions will be produced from God's love and joy. When we are tempted with fearful thoughts, we need to take that thought captive and bring it in line with God's Word. The enemy will tell us that we can't accomplish that task, or that we will fail at that new job, or that it will be too embarrassing to ask for forgiveness. Our response should be that we can do all things through Christ who strengthens us, and we don't agree with those lies. The enemy may be working on some of you reading this book at this very moment. He may be telling you that he is really more powerful than what's being said, but the Word says that greater is He that is in me than he that is in the world (see 1 John 4:4). God lives inside Christians, and He is always with us. So whenever evil thoughts come, remember, God is in you and He is more powerful than Satan. Our sword in this battle is God's Word.

Fear spawns hatred, sadness, and torment. If Satan can get you to fear, he knows that hatred can grow from that fear. The Civil War is a perfect example. During the early days of slavery in the United States, Africans were horribly exploited, raped, and brutally murdered. But why? Were the Africans trying to take over the country? Were the Africans exploiting, raping, and brutally murdering Americans? The reason is fear. Satan had convinced an entire portion of America to fear these slaves. Americans back then were afraid that the slaves were animal like, evil, ignorant, and would take advantage of them at any given opportunity. The result? Inhumane treatment of these slaves that would eventually erupt into civil disorder.

If the enemy can get you to fear, he knows that sadness can grow from that fear. Low self-esteem is a good example. If the enemy can convince you that you are unworthy, strange, ugly, or unappealing in some way, he knows that you will be stifled. He knows that you will develop a low self-esteem and it will be hard for you to develop meaningful relationships. If you don't accept and love yourself, how can you accept and love others? That's why it's important to forgive ourselves when we make mistakes, otherwise the enemy will exploit that mistake in an attempt to lower our self-esteem. He'll say things like, "God didn't really forgive you of that sin, you're unworthy of that kind of forgiveness." And that's when you will say, "When I repent, God is faithful to forgive me. He said so in 1 John 1:9." The enemy also hopes that the sadness will develop into depression. There are millions of Christians walking around depressed and don't even know it. How can Christians, who have Almighty God on their side, be walking around depressed? Because some depressed Christians aren't versed enough in the Word. We suffer for lack of knowledge. Sometimes we have a hard time incorporating spiritual principles. We've all struggled in this area. And just because we know what to do doesn't mean it's easy. It takes commitment and dedication.

We have to be committed to prayer and dedicated to the Word of God. What's hard for us is easy for God. Sometimes the hardest part of our struggles is turning it over to God and, patiently and faithfully, trusting Him to work it out for our benefit. There comes a time when we have to stop trying to fix it ourselves. Satan can never cause us to be sad as long as we know that we are made in God's image and we were created for a specific purpose. God loves us and will never leave us. He is bigger than any problem we have.

If the enemy can get you to fear, he knows that torment can grow from that fear. There are many people who are psychologically tormented every day of they're lives. These individuals' lives are characterized by anxiety. Anxiety, or psychological tension, is the result of fear. Whatever you fear can cause anxiety. Some people fear heights, while others fear darkness. Some people fear spiders, while others fear death. All of us at some point in our lives have feared something and if we perpetuated that fear, chances are we now have an anxiety to that which we feared. Anxieties torment us daily. They keep us captive, they force us to shrink our world, and they weaken us spiritually. I believe that before we go to the psychiatrist for help in dealing with our anxieties, we should go to God. God knows the solution to your problems. God doesn't give us fear, He gives us peace. "For you did not receive a spirit that makes you a slave again to fear, but you received the Spirit of sonship. And by him we cry 'Abba, Father."(Romans 8:15 NIV).

Our heavenly Father watches over us and protects us, and He is greater than that which we fear. We shall have comfort and power in God according to our faith. If your faith in God's promises is not strong, then maybe God has made a way for you through professional assistance. He has the power to guide the doctors on our behalf as well. He has all power. The point is that we do not have to suffer from tormenting anxieties. "Be anxious for nothing, but in everything by prayer and supplication, with thanksgiving, let your request be made known to God." (Philippians 4:6). What are we instructed to do when we feel anxious? We are to go to God in prayer and unload our concerns while being thankful for what He has done for us already.

One of the most common ways we perpetuate anxieties is by worrying. Another way is to ignore them, in which case we just delay the consequences. But worrying is worse in that it actually strengthens fear and anxiety. Worrying is a sin. It is an offense to God to worry. Jesus asked His disciples in Luke 12:25-26 (NIV), "Who of you by worrying can add a single hour to his life? Since you cannot do this very little thing, why do you worry about the rest?" Jesus knew the cycle of fear, which is fear worry anxiety fear. The next time you're tempted to worry about something, remember that by doing so you are offending God and surrounding yourself in fear. God has the solution to fear. Love. "There is no fear in love. But perfect love drives out fear, because fear has to do with punishment." (1 John 4:18 NIV). God is perfect love, and He drives out fear. Fear punishes and torments. Love forgives and heals.

Just for clarification, you may come across passages in the Bible that say, "fear God." The context of fear in these types of statements is reverential. We are to revere or be in awe of God. We are not to be distressed or terrorized by God, that's absurd. You can look up the word "fear" in any credible dictionary and see what I'm talking about. Don't let the enemy confuse you.

V

Jealousy and Envy

Jealousy

Jealousy and envy are often mentioned together. They are often spoken of as interchangeable, but in reality there are some differences worth mentioning. Let's take a closer look at each one. The *Merriam- Webster Dictionary* defines "jealous" as intolerant of rivalry or unfaithfulness. We can identify with a jealous husband or wife, jealousy between children, and jealousy between friends. When one individual feels that someone close to them is being unfaithful in one way or another, jealous feelings can arise. In fact, God is characterized as being jealous. "For the Lord your God is a consuming fire, a jealous God." (Deuteronomy 4:24). God is intolerant of rivalry. He doesn't want you to worship any other god. He is The One True God. God is love, which means that jealousy is a characteristic of love. Another way to describe the relationship between love and jealousy is to say that love comes before jealousy. A husband must first love his wife before he can be jealous towards her. In fact, I've heard stories of women who use jealousy to test a man's love towards them. They feel like if they provoke a man to become jealous, then he must love her because love comes before jealousy. Jealousy is a consuming fire that should not be toyed with. In fact, most humans don't have the wisdom or strength to deal with jealousy. "Anger is cruel and fury overwhelming, but who can stand before jealousy?"(Proverbs 27:4 NIV). It is easy for jealousy to overcome us and consume us in its powerful flames, which is why jealousy is such an attractive force for Satan to use against us. He knows that jealousy is a consuming emotion that we are easily overcome by, which is why we must be very careful when jealous feelings arise. In the Song of Solomon, the bride wrote to her beloved concerning deep love: "Place me like a seal over your heart, like a seal on your arm; for love is as strong as death, its jealousy unyielding as the grave. It burns like blazing fire, like a mighty flame." (Song of Solomon 8:6). This is a true testament to the power of relationships. Love grows in healthy relationships, especially in marriages. Marriage is sacred and, in time, the two become as one. It's the power of love that forges two into one. This is why strong relationships are harmful to the enemy. Ever wonder why most people only have a few close friends? Ever wonder why the divorce rate is so high? Ever wonder why it can be difficult to create and maintain healthy relationships? Obviously there are many aspects involved with maintaining healthy friendships and making marriages work, but the point is that it's no accident that the enemy attacks that which produces love. In summary, love comes before jealousy and jealousy is very powerful and very consuming. We should avoid provoking jealousy because we have trouble standing its fiery flames. The enemy will attempt to provoke us with this emotion because he knows that if we (who can't stand its fiery flames) are forced to deal with it fully, it can be destructive.

Envy

The *Merriam-Webster Dictionary defines* "envy" as painful or resentful awareness of an advantage enjoyed by another, joined by the desire to possess that same advantage. When we want what someone else has, we are envious of them. The last of the Ten

Commandments touched on this. We are not to covet (desire) anything that belongs to our neighbor (see Exodus 20:17). God has given us specific instructions not to envy. It's interesting that the word "painful" appears in the definition of envy. This implies that it hurts us to envy, and that's a pretty good reason to avoid it in the first place. The persons that we envy are unaffected and usually unaware of our envious feelings.

As is the case with jealousy, there is a relationship between love and envy. "Love is patient, love is kind. It does not envy, it does not boast, it is not proud." (Corinthians 13:4 NIV). When we walk in love, we don't have a desire to posses what someone else has because love does not envy. In order to avoid envy, we must increase our love and understanding. We must understand that all good things come from God, and if He has decided to bless our neighbor with a good thing, then it is meant for them to have it. It is God's will. We can't always understand God's will, but we must understand that we must accept it. God blesses whom He chooses to bless, with or without our permission. We may not think it's fair, but we don't have all knowledge. And we should also realize that when God blesses us, there are people who are probably harboring envious thoughts towards us as well. They may think it's unfair that we are enjoying a particular blessing while they aren't. There is probably someone that you may not even know, who is envious of you this very moment. We should be thankful for every little thing that God has blessed us with already. Some of us don't appreciate what we have now, yet we expect God to bless us with more. Before we even open our mouths to ask God for something, we should acknowledge and be thankful for what we already have. "Be anxious for nothing, but in everything by prayer and supplication, with thanksgiving, let your request be made known to God." (Philippians 4:6). And if anyone thinks that they have nothing to be thankful for, I would encourage them to look harder. For if we are alive and have accepted Jesus as our personal Savior, then we have a friend in Jesus. He wants us to obey Him so that we can have a more abundant life here on earth. And one day we will sit with God in heaven and enjoy paradise. God has given us specific instructions about obtaining heavenly blessings (see Deuteronomy 28:1-3). Put simply, if we obey God, He will bless us and He has more than enough to go around.

So we see that although jealousy and envy are usually expressed synonymously, they are different. The most notable aspect that they have in common is their destructive capability. Jealousy is intolerant of rivalry and develops where there is love. Its destructive force is usually directed outward towards the "loved one." Envy desires to have an advantage that someone else enjoys. It develops where love doesn't. Its destructive force is usually directed inward towards the "envious one." In both cases, they are feelings that don't make us happy and full of joy. They are part of the tribulations that we come across in life that must be dealt with properly. In life there will be conflicts and we must deal with them properly.

VI

Overcoming Conflict

Harmony

"These things I have spoken to you, that in Me you may have peace. In the world you will have tribulation; but be of good cheer, I have overcome the world." (John16:33). Jesus has already told us that we will have conflict (tribulation), but He also said that we should cheer up because He has overcome the world. And since we are in Him, and He is in us, that means that we have overcome the world. We are more than conquerors. We have to deal with conflict appropriately or we won't live victoriously. The first step in dealing with conflict is to properly recognize and identify it.

Conflict comes in many different variations. Conflict is basically anything that brings you out of harmony. If you normally live in harmony, it's easy to tell when you're not in it anymore. Unfortunately, most of us are out of harmony to begin with, so conflict is even more difficult to recognize. We get so engulfed in our day-to-day affairs that we don't have time to get or stay in harmony. When I refer to harmony, I'm speaking of being in harmony with God. The only way to get in harmony with God is to get in harmony with His Word (see John 14:6). We must come into agreement with God about how to live our lives. His Word must be the final authority. There are hundreds of commandments throughout the Bible and none of us have kept them all perfectly. We don't have the power to perfect ourselves, only the Word does. And the Word never fails. So, don't avoid coming into harmony with God because you fear that you're not perfect or can't possibly be what He wants you to be. He knows your imperfections better than you do. He wants your attention, and He will handle the rest. He will perfect you in His image. "And we, who with unveiled faces all reflect the Lord's glory, are being transformed into his likeness with ever-increasing glory, which comes from the Lord, who is the Spirit." (2 Corinthians 3:18 NIV). By giving God your attention (meditating on His Word) and coming into obedience with His will, we obtain harmony with Him. Therefore, the way we recognize conflict is by determining if we are outside of God's Word.

The next step in dealing with conflict is to react in obedience to the Word. Once we've identified and recognized that we are out of harmony with God's Word, we need to react. It's not good enough to say, "Yeah, I'm stressed out and confused most of the time, but that's life. This is the price I have to pay to get what I want." The truth is that you shouldn't be stressed out and confused most of the time. God gives you grace to deal with your day-to-day activities, when you are in harmony with His Word. When you are living according to your own ambitions, that's when things can get hectic. Now, I'm not saying that you shouldn't be ambitious, but you should ask God to guide your life so you won't make unnecessary mistakes. Who do you think can guide your life better, you or God? Let's examine some situations where we would normally encounter conflict and discuss some ways we are to handle that conflict.

Conflicts at Home

God wants us to live peaceably with each other, especially

at home. "Better a dry crust with peace and quiet than a house full of feasting, with strife." (Proverbs 17:1 NIV). If we can't find peace in the place where we rest our heads, how much more difficult will it be to find peace throughout the day? We should begin and end our day with peace. And the place where we begin and end our days is at home. As I've mentioned before, I grew up in household that saw two different stepmothers come and go. As a teenager, my stepmother mistreated me in subtle ways. It got to the point where I didn't like to come home. I would stay outside as late as I could, and when I finally came in I would feel awful. It physically made me feel ill to come home to a house that was full of resentment and stress. My attitude at school got worse and I even joined a small gang. I was no angel during those years. Fortunately, this was the time I was developing a habit of reading at least one Bible verse every night. As I developed my relationship with God, I was able to cope with my situation, and eventually God delivered me. Because of my respect for adults, my father in particular, I endured my situation over the years as best I could. Eventually I was accepted at Howard University, and I moved out of my father's apartment in Gary, Indiana. We all go through certain situations for a reason, and I don't regret any of my experiences, especially attending Catholic schools for twelve years. I learned at an early age that hatred only hurts the person that hates, so I was careful not to let my feelings toward my stepmother develop into hatred. Over the years, I've dealt with my feelings towards her, and to this day, I can honestly say that I have forgiven her and I have no resentment in my heart towards her. It took a lot of prayer and growth to get to this point, but I knew I had to get here. Because, as we've discussed, God forgives me of my sins, the way I forgive others who sin against me. Let's review how I dealt with this conflict. At the time I knew, I wasn't living in harmony because I physically felt ill when I would come home. (Recognition and Identification)

Although I didn't know much about the Word at that age, I knew that one of the Ten Commandments was to "Honor my Father and Mother." This was one of the main reasons why I endured my situation. I also knew that God expects us to love everybody, including our enemies, so I never allowed myself to hate my stepmother. (Reaction in Obedience to the Word) My actions were directly guided by the Word and eventually, after much prayer, I was delivered. In summary, we must strive to get along with our family members as best we can and not get caught up in being vengeful and resentful. Our family members hurt us quicker than others because they are so close to us. In the end, we must forgive family members who hurt us for our own sakes and put our trust in God to deliver us.

Conflicts at Work

Conflicts at work are fairly common. Our workforce is more diverse than it's ever been and with diversity comes differences—differences in race, gender, religion, morals, social standing, etc. When we look at all of our differences, it's easy to see why there's so much conflict at work. There are laws in the United States, like many countries, that protect us from discrimination, harassment, and unfair work practices. There are even unions and management bodies dedicated to ensuring fair work practices. Unfortunately, laws, unions, and management can't eliminate conflict in the workplace, nor do they attempt to really. Some conflicts stem from external differences, but many are simply a result of personality conflicts. Our individual ability to manage strife plays a large role in minimizing the amount of conflict we encounter in the workplace. People who are easily angered, impatient, or unwise generally experience more difficulty overcoming conflicts in the workplace. The way we overcome conflict in the workplace is to first look in the mirror. We can't change the fact that there are different types of personalities in the workplace. We can't change the fact that there will be differences of opinion, but we can change our behavior towards our differences.

Let's look at our model for conflict resolution. The first thing we must do is recognize and identify the conflict. When we begin to take our differences personally, that's usually the beginning of conflict. Here's an example: You're leading a team to develop a new thingamabob. You have directed the team to explore certain avenues that you know will produce the results you want, but Trish has a different avenue that she believes is worth exploring. You have no reason to believe that Trish's way won't be successful, but you deny Trish the opportunity to explore her idea because you've already directed the team in another direction. In fact, you deny Trish the opportunity to explore most of her ideas because her ideas are usually contrary to yours. Because of this, you believe Trish is a troublemaker who doesn't like you and is out to make you look foolish. You and Trish are frequently at odds. Can you identify the source of the conflict between you and Trish in this scenario? Is Trish the source of conflict? The conflict began with the assumption that Trish is a troublemaker and has bad intentions towards you. Where did that assumption come from? It came from your mind. It came because you misjudged Trish's God-given ambition and creativity as an attempt to do you harm. Once you are able to recognize that your thought process led you to the false assumption, you are ready to move on to the next step in our conflict-resolution model.

Now that you've identified the source of the conflict, you must react in obedience to the Word. "It is to a man's honor to avoid strife, but every fool is quick to quarrel." (Proverbs 20:3 NIV). The Word says that we should avoid strife for our own honor. Think of a supervisor or manager that you honor and respect. Chances are they are someone who's good at minimizing strife and resolving conflicts. Let Trish explore her idea! What if she discovers an innovative way to develop thingamabobs that earns the company millions of dollars? Trish and her whole team will be recognized. The whole team may even get a bonus. The point is that we should avoid strife by not taking things personally (entertaining false assumptions). If there was a justifiable reason why Trish could not pursue her idea (no funds, no resources, no time, etc.) then it's understandable and prudent to direct Trish down the best path for the team's sake. But if the only reason you're not allowing Trish to explore her ideas is basically because "I said so," then maybe you should evaluate your motives. But what if Trish really was out to make you look foolish? What if Trish really did have bad intentions towards you? The consequence is the same. You should react in obedience to the Word. "Surely he will save you from the fowler's snare." (Psalm 91:3 NIV). As a believer, you have God on your side. So as long as you trust in God, He won't allow any evil plans to trap you or harm you. So there's no need in worrying about who's trying to "get" you because God is watching out for you.

I know this only represents one type of workplace conflict and that workplace conflicts come in all shapes and sizes, but the model for conflict resolution in the workplace doesn't change. We must first identify the source of the conflict, whether it is entertaining false assumptions or some other source. Next, we must react in obedience to the Word, and I'm confident that the Word can address any scenario we can imagine.

Conflicts at Church

You would expect to find the least amount of conflict in the church, but unfortunately it's just the opposite. The church is sacred and has been described as the bride of Christ. "Husbands, love your wives, just as Christ also loved the church and gave Himself for it, that He might sanctify and cleanse it with the washing of water by the word, that He might present it to Himself a glorious church, not having spot or wrinkle or any such thing, but that it should be holy and without blemish. So husbands ought to love their own wives as their own bodies; he who loves his wife loves himself. For no one ever hated his own flesh, but nourishes and cherishes it, just as the Lord does the church." (Ephesians 5:25-29). We, as believers, are the body of Christ and He loves us, as a husband ought to love his wife. Is it any wonder why Satan is out to attack the church and attack it vehemently? He tries to attack those whom God loves. This is why we must be extra vigilant concerning matters of the church.

Conflict can exist between church members in the same way it can exist between family members. Whether the conflict is between a deacon and a pastor or a member and an usher, it's still a destructive element that doesn't belong in the church. Once strife enters the church, it begins to divide the church against itself. And a church divided won't stand long.

The model for conflict resolution applies to the church as well. When the enemy introduces the poison of strife and division we must first recognize that we are being influenced by evil spirits and then we should identify the enemy's plan. For example, you may be developing bad feelings towards the choir director because he doesn't select the songs during service that you would like him to select. You begin to rationalize why he doesn't select the songs that you think he should. Before you come to the conclusion that he's purposely trying to upset you or that he's exhibiting favoritism in some way, you should stop and say to yourself, "Wait a minute, why I am letting the choir director's song selection bother me so much? It's his job to select the songs and his selection is Holy Spirit inspired. Someone in here needed to hear this song at this minute. Satan is behind this and he wants me to be in strife with the choir director. Well, I'm not falling for it and I rebuke you Satan. Leave me alone and don't bother me about this again in Jesus' name." When we rebuke the enemy, we drive him out of our heads. We are also following the second principle of conflict resolution, which is to react in obedience to the Word. And the Word says, "Drive out the mocker and out goes strife; quarrels and insults are ended." (Proverbs 22:10 NIV). Satan is a mocker and he is the real enemy behind the person you are at strife with. Many times we make the mistake of being mad at the one who transgresses against us when in reality that person is being influenced by the mocker, the enemy, the father of lies, Satan. But if we drive out the mocker, then the strife ceases. The best way to keep the enemy's influence at bay is to guard our own individual thoughts and apply these spiritual principles of conflict resolution.

The enemy wants to divide us, period. It doesn't matter to him whether he divides our homes, our businesses, or our churches just as long as he creates division. He's happy because he knows that as long as we are divided we won't come together in full unity in Christ. When we are full of envy, strife, and division we can't grow spiritually. We become stagnant, lukewarm Christians and God is not satisfied with that. We must operate in love and in truth to avoid the separation that the enemy brings. "If it is possible, as far as it depends on you, live at peace with everyone." (Romans 12:18 NIV).

VII

Joy—The Constant in Your Life

As we approach the final section of this book, I hope you realize that happiness is attainable and that it is God's will for you. Joy can be used to incorporate happiness into your life. Joy is a powerful spiritual fruit that sustains us and is emotionally refreshing. When we stay focused on the promises of God, we acquire and maintain joy. Yes, joy must be maintained. If we don't actively stay focused on the Word of God, then our daily trials and tribulations will overcome us. In this section we will also discuss a more assertive way to utilize joy. Finally, we will discuss the ultimate joy of Jesus' return. So let's turn our attention to maintaining joy.

Maintaining Joy

We attain joy by being ever focused on the promises of God through the Word. Unfortunately, the enemy is ever focused on stealing our joy. The good news is that we have a 100-percent-guaranteed security system that the enemy cannot penetrate. Faith in the Word of God will always produce joy. The only way the enemy can steal our joy is when we let our guards down and feed into his lies. Deception is his primary weapon. So when we speak of maintaining joy, we are really talking about walking in truth, which is the Word of God. "Jesus said to him, 'I am the way, the truth, and the life." (John 14:6). So in order to walk in truth, we must not be deceived. How does the enemy create deception? Mainly through fear, worry, and doubt. We've already discussed the pitfalls of fear and worry and their relationship, which is fear→worry→anxiety→fear. This captivating cycle must be broken in order to have joy. How do we break the cycle? By walking in truth. As a little boy, I was afraid of the dark. When the lights went out at bedtime, I would begin to worry about what was hiding in the dark. The more I worried, the more I began to "look" for things. I would stare in the closet and see shapes and figures. I would imagine something being under the bed. It was terrible. Needless to say, I had a hard time falling asleep. It got to the point where I would become full of anxiety at bedtime because of my fear of the dark. It was a vicious cycle. I broke this cycle over the years, by walking in truth. The truth was that a fatigued eye does wonders with shapes in the dark. There are many visual games that can be played on the eyes, especially in the dark. For example, if you stare at a bright red dot for thirty seconds, then look at a white sheet of paper, you'll still see the dot. There are many books on visual illusions that people buy for entertainment. The truth is that a squeaky floor can be a result of settling, worn-out carpet pads, rotting wood, rodents, people walking in another room, heating ductwork under the floor causing expansion of the wood, etc. But what really produces security for me is Psalm 91. Here are some excerpts: "He who dwells in the shelter of the Most High will rest in the shadow of the Almighty. I will say of the Lord, 'He is my refuge and my fortress, my God in whom I trust.' Surely He will save you from the fowler's snare and from the deadly pestilence. You will not fear the terror of night. For He will command His angels concerning you to guard you in all your ways. 'Because he loves me', says the Lord, 'I will rescue him; I will protect him for he acknowledges my name. He will call upon me and I will answer him; I will be with him in trouble I will deliver him and honor him. With long life will I satisfy him and show him my salvation." (excerpts from Psalm 91 NIV). If you believe these words, how can you be afraid of anything? By eliminating the fear, I eliminated the worry and anxiety, and the cycle was broken.

Another way the enemy tries to steal our joy is through doubts. If the enemy can cause you to doubt the promises of God, he can stifle your faith in those promises. Doubt corrodes faith, which is why faith exist where there is no doubt. In fact, one way to define faith is *to have no doubts about that which we believe.* We must accept the Word as the final authority in our lives. If it is written, it is the truth. If we don't understand the Word, we must seek answers through the Holy Spirit. Jesus said, "But the Helper, the Holy Spirit, whom the Father will send in my name, He will teach you all things, and bring to you remembrance all things that I said to you." (John 14:26). So don't allow yourself to doubt the Word. As you read and learn God's Word you will come across some things that you don't understand. Just because something doesn't make sense to you, doesn't mean it's not true. Remember God's understanding is above yours. It may be that you need more understanding to make sense out of what you're reading. You may run across some things that are clear but beyond reason. Just remember that what's written in the Bible is not beyond God's reason, and He can help you accept the Word. Don't make the mistake of thinking that your reasoning makes God's Word true. God's Word is the truth.

Grudges

We've discussed the unbearable price of being unforgiving and how it stifles the work of God in our lives. Because we understand its negative effects, we must not allow ourselves to hold a grudge. This is another way the enemy tries to steal our joy. By constantly bringing to mind the ways in which we've been hurt and the people who have hurt us, the enemy prevents us from experiencing joy. One of the subtle ways we allow ourselves to hold a grudge is by giving someone the silent treatment. Although it may seem like a passive way to get back at someone, it's actually damaging and manipulative. When we make a habit of giving the silent treatment, we make it more difficult to resolve issues and the longer we are in "silent mode" the easier it is for the enemy to negatively influence us. Over time, grudges can ruin communication and conflict resolution in a relationship. Some people use grudges as a manipulative tool to get their way. Not only is this harmful to relationships, it's also selfish. We need to understand that we're not always going to have our way. If there's something that we desire to have, we should ask God for it and let Him work out the details of acquiring it for us instead of taking things into our own hands. God will decide if, when, and how to give us what we desire. God's not going to give us something just because we think we need it. He's our Father and He's not going to give us something that will destroy us, so sometimes you may get your heart's desire instead of your desire in your mind. When we are making a conscious effort to withhold communication and affection in order to get our way or get even, we are actually being manipulative and/or vengeful. As Christians, we are called to be other- centered and not self-centered. We have also been called to practice forgiveness and not harbor vengeful feelings. Be bold and make the decision right now to be aware of when you're holding a grudge and stop it. When you sincerely do that, God's work will be effective in your life, and you will be successful at maintaining your joy.

Guilt

When we talk about guilt, we are usually talking about it in one of two ways. Either we are referring to a state or charge of committing a crime, or we are talking about a feeling of responsibility for an act that goes against our moral code or conscious. From a legal standpoint; we are accused of a crime, tried by a jury, found guilty, convicted of the crime, then suffer our penalty. From a Christian standpoint, we are judged and convicted of our actions (sins) by the Holy Spirit, we repent of our sins, ask for forgiveness, and we are forgiven. Notice that for Christians, there's no guilt. "But, Brian, are you saying that Christians don't experience guilt?" Unfortunately, they do. For a Christian, guilt comes when we don't follow the process all the way through. Let's look at the process again. Conviction comes at the beginning for Christians whereas it comes near the end of the legal process. This is because we are being convicted by the Holy Spirit (perfect) and in the legal process we are being convicted by other human beings (imperfect). The Holy Spirit dwells within Christians and His judgement is perfect. The legal process requires a jury of many people that may or may not pass a fair judgement. The Holy Spirit doesn't need a trial because He was there with us when we committed the sin and knew what was going on in our minds at the time. Once we are convicted by the Holy Spirit, we as Christians are called to repent so that we may be forgiven, redirected, and cleansed of that sin. Once we are convicted (found guilty) of a crime by the legal system, we usually serve some type of penance, such as time in prison. Then where does the guilt come in for Christians? When we don't repent and have faith in God's forgiveness.

To repent means to feel sorrow or remorse for our sins. This means that we have to understand what we did wrong in the first place. We can't be sorry for something we don't realize was wrong.

For some Christians, this is usually where the Holy Spirit comes in. It's the Holy Spirit who convicts us of our sins. Sometimes we realize the Holy Spirit in the form of our conscious (a still, small inner voice). To say that He convicts us is to say that He makes us understand that what we did was sinful and unpleasing to the Lord. As we grow in Christ, we become more sensitive to the Holy Spirit. The Holy Spirit will talk to us like an old friend, and He's always there to convict our hearts, guide us into all truth, and regenerate us. As we mature spiritually, the Holy Spirit will guide us so that we don't commit the sin in the first place. Just who is the Holy Spirit? He is God. God is a triune being: God the Father (Jehovah), God the Son (Jesus Christ), and God the Holy Spirit (The Comforter). One True God.

Satan uses guilt to keep us from coming to God for forgiveness. The father of lies tells us that we don't deserve to be forgiven and that God will never forget our past. Then we feel guilty and live in our sins. We feel unworthy and unloved and as a result we allow our sins to multiply and destroy us. For the end result of sin is death. That's what happens when we listen to Satan. What does God have to say about this? "Let us therefore come boldly before the throne of grace, that we may obtain mercy and find grace in the time of need." (Hebrews 4:16). God instructs us to come boldly to him for mercy and grace (favor and strength). Does that sound like we don't deserve God's forgiveness? God also says, "I, even I, am He who blots out your transgressions for My own sake; And I will not remember your sins." (Isaiah 43:25). Does that sound like God will never forget our past? He is faithful in forgiving us. He is a better forgiver than we are sinners. When the Holy Spirit convicts us of sin, His purpose is to save us and not to condemn us. "When we are judged by the Lord, we are being disciplined so that we will not be condemned with the world." (1 Corinthians 11:32 NIV). Therefore we have no reason to allow guilt to contaminate our lives. Because God protects us, comforts us, leads us into all truth, forgives our sins, and regenerates us, we are to be fear free, worry free, doubt free, grudge free, and guilt free so that we can maintain our joy.

Utilizing Joy

We've discussed acquiring joy through the promises of God and maintaining joy by relying on God to edify us so that the enemy cannot steal the joy we've acquired. God also wants us to utilize our joy so that we become spiritually assertive. Now we will discuss ways to put our joy to work for us. We are more than conquerors in Christ and God has made joy available for us to use not just passively, but assertively. One of the most important tools we have available to us as Christians is prayer, so let's start by discussing how we can utilize joy in prayer.

Pray with Joy

God has given us the invitation to petition Him, cast all our cares upon Him, and even obtain salvation through prayer. Prayer is an important aspect of Christian life that should be performed at least daily. In order for prayer to be effective, we must openly talk to God and exercise faith. Since we are to cast all our cares upon Him, there are many different reasons we pray. Sometimes we pray to ask God for something we need while other times we pray because we are burdened with a problem. We may not always feel joyful when we are praying, but the key to prayer is faith. If we pray without faith, then we are just making noise. We must believe that God will hear our petitions, comfort us, and deliver us from evil. In other words, we must believe that our prayers will be answered. King David, who wrote many songs and prayed often, had this to say about prayer: "I will call on you, O

God, for you will answer me; give ear to me and hear my prayer." (Psalm 17:6 NIV). David didn't pray to God to vent, he prayed because he knew God would answer him. After we have prayed, we should be joyful because God will answer us! We should feel better after we have prayed than we did before we started. We should be joyful because we know our help is coming. Our joy should be the evidence of our faith. "I will be glad and rejoice in Your mercy, For You have considered my trouble." (Psalm 31:7). When we have truly put our trust in God, it is easy to get excited because all-powerful God is going to take up our fight. He is going to work out our bad situation so that it becomes good. He won't fail, He won't forget, and He'll be there the next time.

Generosity

Most of us know that it is better to give than to receive, but God is also concerned about how we give. "Each man should give what he has decided in his heart to give, not reluctantly or under compulsion, for God loves a cheerful giver." (2 Corinthians 9:7 NIV). When we give because we want to give, we feel good about it. We should pay our tithes with joy because we are being obedient to God's Word and we are advancing the prosperity of the church. God has also made promises to those who tithe. "Bring the whole tithe into the storehouse, that there may be food in my house. Test me in this, says the Lord God Almighty, and see if I will not throw open the floodgates of heaven and pour out so much blessing that you will not have room enough for it." (Malachi 3:10 NIV).

We should be full of joy whenever we give to those in need. Jesus tells the story of when He shall return in His full glory in the book of Matthew. *"Then the King will say to those on His right hand, 'Come, you blessed of My Father, inherit the kingdom prepared for you from the foundation of the world: for I was hungry and you gave Me food; I was thirsty and you gave Me drink; I was a stranger and you took Me in; I was naked and you clothed Me; I was sick and you visited Me; I was in prison and you came to Me.' Then the righteous will answer Him, saying, 'Lord, when did we see You hungry and feed You, or thirsty and give You drink? 'When did we see you a stranger and take You in, or naked and clothe You?' 'Or when did we see You sick, or in prison, and come to You?' And the King will answer and say to them, 'Assuredly, I say unto you, inasmuch as you did it to one of the least of these My brethren, you did it to Me.'"* Doesn't it feel good to know that when you are being generous to someone in need, you are being generous to God?

When we give to the poor we should be full of joy because we are helping someone in need and it is pleasing to God. God has also made promises to those who give to the poor. "He who has pity on the poor, lends to the LORD, And He will pay him back what he has given." (Proverbs 19:17). Who better to repay a loan that you gave than God? Surely God's promises indicate that He loves those who take joy in giving and He shows them favor.

Random Acts of Kindness

God has promised that we shall reap what we sow, so why not sow seeds that will bring joy into our lives? If it would fill you with joy for people to show you kindness, favor, goodwill, and love, then why not show others kindness, favor, goodwill, and love? We already know that we'll reap what we sow. If we are throwing good seed around every day and all over the place, that's the way we will receive the benefits of those seeds—every day and all over the place. I remember when I first put this to the test. I was driving to work, and I made up my mind that I was going to be a courteous driver all day long. I allowed people to get in my lane. I didn't tailgate anyone, and I didn't even get upset when someone cut me off. I actually felt good about being able to be a courteous driver for a whole day. That alone was an accomplishment for me. Things changed for me immediately. People would wave me in their lane when I needed to switch lanes. People who were tailgating me would back off almost as soon as I noticed them in my rearview mirror. People would actually give me the hand wave to thank me for letting them in my lane. It was like I was in the twilight zone. It actually worked! I was so excited. I felt like I had some type of control over my circumstance. Needless to say this made my commute more enjoyable. I was ready to throw some more good seeds around whenever the opportunity arose. Whether I had sown good seeds during my commute, on my job, and even at home, the result was always the same. Good fruit would blossom. So bring joy to others by being kind, and others will bring joy to you. Practice random acts of kindness starting today!

Facing Trials

I know that discussing trials and tribulation in the Joy section of this book seems out of place, but there is joy to be gained when we face trials. "Consider it pure joy, my brothers, whenever you face trials of many kinds, because you know that the testing of your faith develops perseverance." (James 1:2-3 NIV). When we look at the big picture, we realize that everything we go through fits into God's ultimate design. Life is a growth process. Every trial that we went through taught us something or gave us something. I challenge you to write down two of the toughest trials of your life. Make a list under each trial. See if you can list three things that you've either learned or gained from each trial. Once you look over your list and appreciate what you've learned, you may even be glad (or full of joy) you experienced the trial in the first place. A reflection of Abraham Lincoln's life illustrates this point really well. He had failed as a businessman more than once. He was defeated when he ran for state legislator, the Senate, and

Congress. He even had a nervous breakdown, yet he was elected president of the United States and is admired for his wisdom and intellect. He learned to persevere through his circumstance. No doubt some of his wisdom and intellect was formed during his trials and tribulations. Had he not gone through those trails, he would not have grown to be the man he developed into. That's why were told to "consider it pure joy" in the book of James. It may not seem like it at the time, but everything works for our benefit and growth. "And we know that all things work together for good to those who love God, to those who are called according to His purpose." (Romans 8:28). If you're facing a trial today, be joyful because what you're gaining is priceless.

Ultimate Joy

The ultimate joy for Christians will be when Jesus returns. Although we may not be fully able to explain what this will feel like, we do know that we will rejoice and be exceedingly glad. Jesus told us, "A woman giving birth to a child has pain because her time has come; but when her baby is born she forgets the anguish because of her joy because a child is born into the world. So now it is with you: Now is your time of grief, but I will see you again and you will rejoice, and no one shall take away your joy." (John 16:21-22 NIV). Nothing can take away our joy when we focus on the fact that eventually we will be with Jesus. Even death is not discouraging when we think of what comes next—fellowship with God Himself. When we are with God in heaven, there'll be no more suffering or sins and all truth will be revealed. It will be a time of exceeding joy. All of the difficulties of this life will cease. No matter what you have gone through or what you are going through now, it can't even be compared to what God has in store for us. Christians should always be aware of the ultimate joy that is their inheritance. We should walk around knowing that there is a beautiful end, which is a beginning, to this life, as we know it. We should enjoy this life fully and expect to enjoy life after physical death. We should heed the instruction of 1 Thessalonians 5:16 (NIV), which says simply, "Be joyful always."

A FINAL NOTE

Congratulations! You made it through the whole book, and I believe that your life will never be the same again. Life is a process and we are constantly learning. As long as we continue to be led by the Holy Spirit, challenge our behavior, and be open to change, we cannot fail in becoming who God wants us to be. I believe this transformation begins with a relationship with God, because He is our Creator and He knows us better than we know ourselves. The way we begin and maintain a relationship with God is through his Word, who is Jesus Christ. The Bible is a book whereby we can experience the Word. To grow in our knowledge of the Bible is to grow in our knowledge of God and growth takes time.

This book covered an array of issues that Christians face every day. These issues are stumbling blocks, which hinder happiness, for many Christians. But rest assured that happiness is God's will for Christians. Happiness is a journey and not a destination. Life presents us with many choices. Day by day, what we choose shapes our destiny. God has provided all the tools we need to choose blessings, prosperity, and eternal life. He has given us everything we need to overcome fear and conflict. As we renew our minds with spiritual principles instead of worldly principles, we bring joy into our lives. Joy is available to all Christians in abundance, and it can be a constant in our lives as we learn how to maintain and utilize it. I hope that this book helped to expose popular misconceptions about happiness because there is a difference between world happiness and true happiness. I also hope that you have been given some insight on conquering those negative giants in your life that are rooted in fear. It is my prayer that you press on with patience and reliance on God for your strength. Nothing is impossible with God. If you have decided to begin a relationship with God, then now is the time to make Jesus the Lord of your life. Say out loud this simple prayer with me now:

> *"Heavenly Father, I come to you now in the Name of Jesus. I believe in your Word, who is Jesus Christ. Your Word says in Romans 10:9-10 and 13 'If you confess with your mouth the Lord Jesus and believe in your heart that God has raised Him from the dead, you will be saved. For with the heart one believes to righteousness and with the mouth confession is made to salvation. For whoever calls upon the name of the Lord shall be saved.' I confess that Jesus is Lord, and I believe in my heart that God raised Him from the dead. I am saved! Jesus is the Lord of my life and I am a Christian. Amen."*

You have chosen life and the angels in heaven are rejoicing. You are God's righteousness and your growth in Christ begins now. Make it a habit to read the Bible every day, even if it's just one verse. Some inspirational websites will send a Bible verse directly to your E-mail every day. I recommend the Kenneth Copeland Ministries at www.kcm.org. If you haven't already done so, find a church home where you can praise God and have fellowship with other Christians. I thank God for you, and I would like you to know that you made the right choice. Happiness is yours.

REFERENCES

1. Merriam-Webster Online Dictionary copyright 2004 by Merriam-Webster, Inc.
2. The Random House College Dictionary copyrights 1984, 1982, 1980, 1979, and 1975 by Random House, Inc.
3. BibleGateway.com copyright 1995-2003 by Gospel Communications International.

www.ingramcontent.com/pod-product-compliance
Ingram Content Group UK Ltd.
Pitfield, Milton Keynes, MK11 3LW, UK
UKHW040031200726
13854UKWH00001B/458